WHEN THE WATER SMOKES

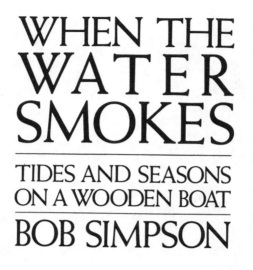

WHEN THE WATER SMOKES

TIDES AND SEASONS ON A WOODEN BOAT

BOB SIMPSON

ALGONQUIN BOOKS *of* CHAPEL HILL

1990

Published by
Algonquin Books of Chapel Hill
Post Office Box 2225
Chapel Hill, North Carolina 27515-2225

a division of
Workman Publishing Company, Inc.
708 Broadway
New York, New York 10003

Library of Congress Cataloging-in-Publication Data
Simpson, Bob, 1925–
When the water smokes : tides and seasons on a wooden boat / Bob Simpson.
p. cm.
ISBN 0-945575-44-0 : $8.95
1. Peltier Creek (N.C.)—Description and travel. 2. Peltier Creek (N.C.)—Social
life and customs. 3. River life—North Carolina—Peltier Creek. 4. Peltier Creek
Valley (N.C.)— Description and travel. 5.Atlantic Coast (U.S.)—Description and
travel. 6. Simpson, Bob, 1925–   —Journeys—North Carolina—Peltier Creek.
I. Title.
F262.P35S57   1990
975.6'197—dc20   90-30947
                   CIP
10 9 8 7 6 5 4 3 2 1

CONTENTS

ACKNOWLEDGMENTS

It was suggested that I dedicate this book to my "typist, helpmeet, and critic, who from the evidence of the manuscript has a great deal to put up with." Thinking it over, I must agree, for without my chief cook and navigator I wouldn't have made it past the first shoals. While I am accused of putting her through much hardship, it is I who has suffered—from her pushing me at times of weakness into such foolishness as buying boats we don't need, going a-wandering just to see what's there, and otherwise keeping me from tending to business and thereby becoming successful. Actually, this book is all her fault: I wrote it, but she made me do it.

There are many other persons without whose help, interest, and encouragement we'd never have undertaken it: readers of my columns in the Raleigh, North Carolina, *News and Observer* over the years who have asked, "Why don't you write a book?" The editors of that newspaper, in publishing most of my submissions, pumped up my ego, often when it was most needed.

There are the waterfront characters, tall and short, good and bad, whom I consider the real people of this world, the Promise Landers and other watermen. Susan and Bill Simpson, my sister-in-law and brother, stood many watches for us, while Bette and Royal Brunson provided us the hideaway we needed for finishing the book. Bill Collins made a fine pen-and-ink drawing of *Sylvia II* that appears herein. Finally, this would never have come to pass without Louis Rubin, who insisted that we could deliver and showed us how.

Bob Simpson
Peltier Creek
Morehead City, N.C.

WHEN THE WATER SMOKES

THE GREAT GROUND
HOG DAY STORM

Rafts of waterfowl lay in the lee of a long shoal, bobbing lightly on the uneasy gray waters. A moderate nor'easter scudded lead-colored clouds above the horizon and a cold mist fogged the indistinct meeting of sky and water. The faded yellows, browns, and greens of the Outer Banks, mere sand ridges meagerly protected by grasses and scrub growth, were low and frail before the thunder of a stormy surf pounding against the winter-washed sands. The Carolinas coast in winter is somber, harsh, and unforgiving. Settled deep in a windrow under a camouflage poncho that gave some shelter from the icy air, I could see a great blue heron probing the marsh edges. What could it find, what minnow so insensitive as not to seek the deep warmth of a channel bottom? A skein of snow geese whistled in from behind me, banked and reversed into the wind to drop in a clamor of greetings between a raft of swans and another of Canada geese. The new arrivals paddled in small circles and, one by one, relaxed, dozing and bobbing in a little bay. Laughing gulls and black skimmers stood on a shoal with shoulders hunched, facing into the wind. There was a scattering of other birds: redheads rafting aloofly farther offshore; red-winged blackbirds clinging to the marsh grasses, swaying precariously in the wind; myrtle warblers holding to the shelter of scrub bayberries.

Except for duck hunters and a few others equally foolish, the seacoast in winter is known but to a fortunate few. The revelry and crowds of summer are long gone. Gone, too, is the joyous, festive feeling one finds in the holiday moods of November and December. Now the candle of life is burning at its lowest ebb. The burned-out ashes of summer have mingled with ice, but the glow of a seasoned fire remains. Summer visitors have faded before the test of cold, leaving winter as the time of closeness, for things most valued and trusted. Summer is noise. Winter is quiet to the point of silence. It is a sparkling clean time to clear mind and air, to turn to one's inner resources, to harden as nature does in thinning out that which is unfit to survive and reproduce and compete for the next year. And the Moon of Hunger will replace the waning Wolf Moon.

On every ice-encrusted sandbar hungry gulls huddle in starving flocks, shivering before the cutting wind. Where are the gay days of wheeling in the soft summer air, of living off the abundant refuse of generous fishermen, boats, and nets? Now the food is deep, hiding in the warmer bottoms or far at sea, no longer in the plenty of littered beach and hot dog stand. Winter is nature's method of returning to the realities of life, perhaps as recession or depression is to man. There comes a time of reckoning, a time when the devil demands his due.

As for myself, certain things have eluded me. There's that big bass. Oh, I've seen him. He is there for the catching, but so far he has evaded me. It's my own fault: I found the chase of some other dream more tempting at the moment. It's like never having got around to building my own boat (a pram built from a kit doesn't count). I still have this upwelling of desire whenever I see a particularly beautiful vessel, or read a ship chandler's catalog. But I'm always torn as to direction: shall it be a steam tug with brass whistle and black stack, or shall it be a spritsail skiff, fast and beautiful, that, as Josh Bailey puts it, will sail on a heavy dew with the belch of a squirrel? Of such are my winter dreams.

After a while, though, cabin fever sets in and this dreamer must return to reality. Then one of the better cures is an outing under our own power, by paddle or oar. My wife Mary and I took the paddle-power cure one blustery day, setting out across Bogue Sound from Peltier Creek, the place that we call home.

The creek is on the fringes of Morehead City, a typical small seacoast town that, like many others, has become increasingly popular as a tourist resort. It all started back before the Civil War, when the town was known as Shepard's Point and one John Motley Morehead decided to run a tourist-transporting rail line to the coast so that upstaters could escape the oppressive summer heat.

Today the community is scarcely recognizable as the pleasant sleepy village of friendly people that I first discovered years ago. On the other side of the Newport River estuary is Beaufort, one of the oldest North Carolina seats of government, for a county—Carteret—that has more water area than land. Across the sound from our cottage lies Bogue Banks, accessible only by water until the 1930s, but favored as a beach resort when the only transportation was a sailing sharpie or a row skiff.

Two hundred years ago the county had a few small plantations, but was mainly a community of fishermen-farmers, with whaling an exciting sideline for those who lived on the Banks. Even a hundred years ago it was virtually unchanged, except for a shortage of whales. With the post–World War II era the tourists began to stay. Useless beach property has soared from no value to thousands per front foot. When the whales show up today, they usually wash ashore dead or dying, and scientists get a chance to examine them before the residents complain about aromas that no longer smell like money.

Little Peltier Creek was the site of a predepression real estate boom that burst. Now almost lost in the backwash of expansion, it is no longer just the haven of a few fishermen and a "hurricane hole." It, too, has felt the impact of growth. Still, in winter it's mostly ours.

The bow of our canoe lifted and sliced through the waves. A damp, bitter wind burned against our faces. Occasionally spray tossed over the sides. The sound had the brilliant metallic glitter of winter, set-

3

ting off the cold blue of the sky, the purity of white clouds and the clear yellow-green of the shallows.

Holding the canoe into the wind, digging the paddles deep, we had left the sanctuary of the creek for a session of corkscrewing, bobbing, twisting, dodging droplets of spray. We made our way into the lee of Cricket Island, skirting oyster rocks and sliding onto a mud flat. Mary stepped out into muck, and I followed, lifting the canoe high and dry to await our return. Pulling up our hip boots, we began to comb the submerged flats. Underfoot was the crunch of oyster shells, cast upon the shoal, drying in sun and wind. There were mosses and seaweeds, salt grasses half submerged, bowing not to the wind but to the current. The rippled sandy bottom told its own story of tidal shaping. We felt the press of water from the ebbing tide, the scouring, the rushing to exits through narrow channels, the easier motion across the flats. Loosened seaweed rolled and tumbled. Mirrored on quieter waters were racing white clouds in a blue sky.

The waterways, almost abandoned by boats, stretched out of sight beyond the horizon. Tiny spoil islands rose to dot the wet with spots of dry sands bleaching in the sun's path. A cluster of white and gray shorebirds rested, all facing into the wind, but rose as one when we approached. Mary filled her hands with shells, empty homes abandoned as their occupants' turn in this world was over, yet to be reused again and again, their architectural skill a surviving monument. A sailboat cruised by smartly, quiet but for her popping jib and the laughter of her wind-bitten crew.

The temperature was falling. Dampness penetrated our clothing as the wind picked up. The conchs remained well hidden. The western sky had a yellow-orange glow. The shadows were long and thin by the time we had called the dog and shoved off. The wind favored us now. A flotilla of mallards spotted us and took flight. A half-dozen disappeared down the sound, but twenty or thirty dropped around us to form an escort. I felt as honored as a returned circumnavigator, but only for a moment. They were simply looking for a handout, quacking loudly as we entered the creek. When I lifted the canoe to my shoul-

4

ders, they formed a column bound for the corn supply. Mary sprinted to the house to revive the fire and put on the coffee.

〰〰〰〰〰〰〰〰〰〰〰

Halfway to spring it becomes necessary, as in the days of our forefathers, to assess one's worth, not in bank accounts, but by the size of the woodpile. The modest fisherman's cottage we call home is old. It sags a bit at the joints and is heated almost entirely by a cast-iron Franklin stove, with a little assistance from the kitchen range. The latter is a relic we found over at Johnny Wetherington's marine railways. It was cast so long ago by the Shipmate Foundry in Stamford, Connecticut, that the company can find no record of ever having made Model 562. It can be fired by propane, wood, or coal, and is designed with sea rails to keep pots and pans from sliding off, and bolt-down legs to prevent its coming adrift in a seaway.

There is a special security, when rain and wind are slatting against the windows and moaning down the chimney, when the bay is covered with gray-bearded combers and the forecast is for cold and colder, in watching the flames dance across a hefty oak log in the open fire. With the aroma of baking beans or bread coming from the kitchen, the acrid odor of hot stove iron has an added appeal. Ingredients like a few juniper twigs tossed onto the coals, buttered popcorn, steaming mulled wine, a good book, perhaps a little light music, the dog dozing on the old bearskin rug, increase the confidence that when the sleet storm levels the power lines and the oil trucks can't get through, we will remain warm and secure, no matter how the winds blow.

In some agricultural societies, particularly in New England, a man's success was measured by the height of his woodpile come Ground Hog Day. But then, we human animals do have peculiar standards of achievement. There are those who collect women, and have them stashed away here and there, and I suppose some women do likewise with males. Others build monuments to themselves, some in the form of houses and estates. One man told me that his goal is to have a tombstone so big that everyone who comes into the county will notice it, thinking it's a lighthouse. When tourists get close, they'll say, "That Cap'n Jack must've been real important!"

Whenever Jack thinks about it, he leans back in his chair, stretches out straight, folds his hands over his belly, sighs and closes his eyes in contentment, as if ready for burial. But he'd better get to building soon, because a monument like the one he has planned will take a lot of bricks. While he contemplates his project, I look upon my woodpile and see it melting. It brings on a kind of despair for the future, mine mostly, especially when the day is one of the miserable kind that produces neither a bona fide rain or a good snow, when the sun's on vacation and gray clouds reign over a cold, raw land, and the wind is moaning in the pines. And if it's around the first of February, I find myself evaluating the oak and cherry and gum in the lee of the shop and remembering the Great Ground Hog Day Storm of 1976.

The weather of January through March is the least predictable, yet in a sense it can be counted on. North Carolina's most severe storms, excepting hurricanes, generally occur during this period. The first of February, 1976, saw the storm forming, and it swept the coast all through the night, moving northeast later on Ground Hog Day. It had made up off the Carolina Capes, somewhere between Fear and Romain. Fishermen and sailors first noticed the barometer falling a little more than seemed reasonable for an optimistic forecast of light and variable winds. The radio was droning, "Ten percent chance of rain and partly cloudy," when *Credence*, a stout Bahama yawl, went out of the creek. My brother Bill was aboard and hailed us, "Going to the Cape. Maybe Shackleford. Be back tomorrow." A light sou'west breeze rippled the sound and barely filled the sails.

Far offshore a convoy of ships was bringing Marines back from a Mediterranean cruise. An anxious commander watched the steady plunge of the barograph. It looked ominous, despite no forecast of a disturbance, and he made the decision to secure all ships for heavy weather and open formation for more ease of navigation.

Along the waterfronts, some watermen had noticed the decline, and the more prudent had put out extra lines and secured hatches. Most folks rely now on the fair-mouthed TV forecaster for observations;

6

few ever notice a barometer. A small schooner had recently arrived from up North. Not liking the looks of the weather, the young couple aboard headed for the basin in Beaufort that the Corps of Engineers had dredged as a harbor of refuge. They tied up alongside a large trawler at a fish dock there. In Morehead City another trawler had been secured at the Texaco dock, opposite Sugarloaf Island, which provides shelter to the waterfront. Among the charter fleet skippers, Cap'n Theodore Lewis eyed his *Sylvia II* and, figuring she was safe enough for the night, went home to reassure his wife.

Offshore, seas were growing, and we could hear the surf building against the beach. Still the air was warm, winds only light sou'west when we left to join friends at an oyster roast in Norm Gillikin's Down East backyard. The mist was incidental, and a light, passing patter of rain was ignored while oysters popped and snapped over the driftwood fire. When we returned home that evening and noted the continuing downward course of the barometer, we began to wonder about Bill and *Credence*. But we calmed ourselves: the owner, ex-submariner Lex Mathews, and his crew were experienced, and they must have noticed the falling glass. Besides, the Hook of the Cape gives plent · of protection, especially inside Wreck Point. Did Lex know about that anchorage? Surely Bill did—he's pretty cautious. Still, we felt uneasy.

Even two miles from the beach, we could hear the seas exploding on the strand through the night as the wind picked up steadily. All across the county, boats were being slammed and pounded, lines chafing, parting. Hulls beat against docks, pilings and one another, while skippers and crews fought to save them. The schooner in Beaufort's storm harbor was battered almost to pieces, and the crew could scarcely scramble from their sinking boat to the decks of the trawler. Cap'n Burlon Pittman, awakened by increasing winds, had hurried from his home to check on the trawler at the Texaco dock. Gale winds and heavy seas were pounding her to death, but he had to stand by, unable to get aboard.

From the seawall in Morehead City Cap'n Theodore watched helplessly as his *Sylvia II* slammed repeatedly on a piling until, stove in, she sank. In Cape Lookout Bight, where *Credence* had anchored, not behind Wreck Point, but behind the sand spit that forms the Hook of the Cape, the water had been "slick ca'am," as natives say. Yet between ten P.M. and one A.M., the wind had reached full gale. Long before first light the winds were of hurricane force, and the seas in the bight were nine feet. During that seemingly endless night *Credence* lost her mains'l, which had been tightly furled. The tiller, though tied down, broke, and the mizzenmast gave way.

Not until daylight did the storm begin to ease, dropping to perhaps thirty-five knots. From the tower Coast Guardsmen had watched the little boat, unable to go to her assistance. As soon as the wind decreased, Chief Styron dispatched a boat to carry the crew ashore and restore them with hot coffee.

Later that day the command ship of the convoy came into the port of Morehead City and was met by ambulances to transfer eight crewmen to the hospital. They had been injured when a huge sea stove in the bridge, fifty-five feet above the waterline.

During the early morning hours the storm was racing north'ard past the Virginia Capes to wreak its fury on Georges Bank and Newfoundland, where a score or so vessels were badly beaten, several disappearing without a trace. One of Bill's companions on board *Credence*, former Marine Bob Davis, commented, "What would it have been if a storm had been forecast?" Perhaps only the National Weather Service has the answer, but as any old timer around here will tell you, the Carolina Capes can breed their own hurricanes.

∞∞∞∞∞∞∞∞∞∞∞∞∞

Mary and I were walking the waterfront after the blow when we came upon Theodore, gazing sadly at the broken, oil- and mud-covered remains of his boat, trying to salvage what he could of the equipment, mumbling about the citation he'd just received from polluting the harbor with oil and gasoline from his sunken craft. We'd always liked Theodore and *Sylvia II*, last of the old-time party boats left on the waterfront. Her loss seemed the end of an era. Sympathizing, we, too, took up gazing at the pile of debris, torn planks, oil-soaked life jackets, broken glass.

I found myself remembering the good days of the old waterfront as we first knew it, of skippers like Darcy Willis, "Long Charlie" Willis, Joe Rose, Dave Gould, Auldin Guthrie, Johnny Guthrie, those who were hanging around the waterfront when we came there shortly after World War II. And the boats that came and went: "Pappy Joe" Fulcher's *Lualma* was the oldest boat in the harbor. Originally a sailboat, her keel had been laid the same year that "Pappy" was conceived. (When "Pappy" died, in his late eighties, so did *Lualma*.) Johnny Styron had a trim craft, also named *Sylvia*. Like *Sylvia II*, she carried parties to fish the inlet, the beaches, the jetty, and the shoals of Cape Lookout.

In those days Bill Styron ran the Gulf dock. He kept a bottle in a sea boot, and every boatman on the Inland Waterway from Boston to Brownsville knew Bill and the bottle and the sea boot. Skippering a party boat then meant cooking breakfast on board before setting sail. It was said that never had the waterfront smelled so good as when predawn chefs prepared fish and hot biscuits for their parties. Chances were the boat would anchor for lunch in the Hook of the Cape, long enough for cooking the bluefish that had just been caught over the Cape Shoals. That's how more than one waterfront restaurant got its start, places like the Sanitary where, customers claimed, Ted Garner and Tony Seamon were better cooks than fishermen. And Bill Ballou abandoned his *Victory* for a waterfront café that had once been a fish house. Only Cap'n Ottis Purifoy stuck with fishing, but maybe he simply couldn't cook.

We commiserated with Theodore. "What're you gonna do now? Think she can be salvaged?"

"Mebbe, but I'm too old for that kind of work now . . . just don't know . . . she ain't worth much."

I walked down a pier alongside her. She was badly stove in forward, and her stern was torn up. I'd always thought of her as beautiful; graceful lines, too. "Maybe you could sell her," I suggested. "I've always liked her . . . seems a shame to let her go." If the stern wasn't in too bad shape, and the hole forward could be repaired, maybe the old girl would float again, I thought.

Theodore looked at me. "Two hundred bucks and she's your problem."

I was stunned. Me? I staggered from the shock. "Two hundred bucks! You sure?" He had a fish on, but only he knew it. He nodded, "It's a deal."

My conscience spoke up: "It's a steal! But give the poor guy time." Aloud, I answered, "Tell you what, Theodore, it's a deal, but I'll give you till tomorrow to reconsider." Mary and I needed time, too, though we didn't talk about it much that evening. We rarely do on big decisions: "Suits me if it suits you." But we can debate forever on trifles.

By no means wealthy, we are extremely adept at impulse buying. The idea of such a good deal took all precedence over possible costs. Our discussions were limited to: "Can it be patched?" "Hope so." "Reckon the engine is salvageable?" "Maybe." There was no negativism in our thoughts: "It's purty. I like it." "Well, let's go!"

Next morning, checkbook in hand, we set off to see Theodore, but with some apprehension. I kept thinking, a little belatedly, What do I need with another boat? I couldn't afford the dockage on the last one we had. Maybe she can't even be salvaged. What will it really cost? But Theodore was ready for us. "I been thinkin' it over," he mumbled. "Things are sorta rough now. Could you make it four hundred?"

It was our chance to sober up and back out, but I made a counter offer. "Three hundred, and another hundred if the engine can be saved."

Next thing I knew, Theodore, stuffing a check into his pocket, was looking sadder and saying, "Take good care of her, and maybe when you get her fixed up we'll all go fishin' together." He walked away, and someone else said, "Congratulations!" I felt like a new father, of what I wasn't exactly sure. But the cold shock of ownership of still another boat (after moving ashore, we'd been pained to have to part with the aging cruiser *Silver Spray*, our home for 18 years) was soon replaced by a mingling of fright and anticipation, nightmare and quavering pride. We were now the bewildered proprietors of a hulk full of mud, oil, splinters, torn canvas, and shattered glass.

Cap'n Tony didn't consider that a sunken boat and all the debris alongside the restaurant was good for business, and wanted *Sylvia II* moved as soon as possible. I tried to assess the damage: besides the distribution of mud and oil all the way to whatever was left of the cockpit canopy, the hole in the hull went from the waterline through the deck and cabin side on the forward port quarter. The stern was badly chafed, the cabin twisted, the portholes smashed. Otherwise she was in good shape for having been sunk.

It hadn't been too much of a job to get her off the bottom, with the willing hands that are to be found on waterfronts. With plywood and a plastic tablecloth nailed over the gaping hole in her bow, a big pump had made relatively short work of emptying her, for at low tide and in a shallow slip most of her cockpit was exposed. As the tide had risen, so had *Sylvia II*.

We prowled along the seawall looking for missing parts such as hatch covers, life jackets, and floorboards, without much success. I called on my brother Bill, now fully recovered from his ordeal in the same storm that had sunk *Sylvia II*, to tow her with his little cruiser. With a nervous crew watching, and hoping that the patches would hold, we headed down the Intracoastal Waterway in a raw winter wind towards the marine railway in Peltier Creek.

Increasingly confident that the patch would stay on, I let my dreams take shape: with luck, by summer *Sylvia II* would be restored to her former glory, as she was when party boating was a family affair forty and fifty years before. Hers would be a proper restoration, I vowed, with none of this plastic and fiberglass artificiality over her honest, solid heart of pine and juniper. A museum piece, she would cruise the sounds recapturing, enlivening the past. As I steered in the wake of my brother's boat, I was wallowing in nostalgia. I just couldn't help daydreaming of the refurbishing of this fine craft. It called for split bamboo rods, vintage reels, and any old-style equipment. What she needed most was a classic cast iron Shipmate galley range, like the one we used to have on *Silver Spray*. That was a tiny wood- and coal-burner that would fry a mackerel or bake a flounder. We would look for anything befitting a sea-going small boat of the twenties and thirties, such as gimbaled kerosene lamps and loon-bone lures that caught old-fashioned, unsophisticated mackerel.

By the time we had reached the yard, I could see her, all decked out in shining white and buff, with her graceful round stern and round cabin, flying the house flag from the spreader and signal flags fluttering fore and aft of the mast. She'd carry the Stars and Stripes, rather than the yacht ensign, as befits a lady of her stature, for she is documented in the coasting trade and mackerel fishery. On a day sweetly pungent with scents of tar and salt, she'd slide easily through the chop in golden sunlight glittering off the sound, with a deep-throated "pocketa-pocketa" as her slow-turning engine throbbed quietly. Sitting aft, wearing his salty skipper's cap, would be Cap'n Theodore, along for the ride, taking the wheel only if he felt like it. *Sylvia II* would be queen of the waterfront, a tribute to a special breed of party boat skippers. I might even slip on a steam whistle for effect, but in the meantime I would have to settle for some juniper planks and a reliable bilge pump.

Boatyards stimulate such reveries. They represent a way of life in coastal Carolina, in the scent of cedar shavings, of paint and varnish, mingled with odors of the sea, of turpentine and tar. It may be a half-framed boat under a shed or beneath the canopy of a sprawling live oak, the hammering, the rasping of saws as someone's dream gradually takes form. Or it may be the patient planing of a plank, the careful adzing of a timber into a true and straight keel or stem, the slap of a paint brush. It is enhanced by the lazy stare of gulls on pilings near the shore, in the marsh grasses' rustling, the white egrets' stalking the shallows.

Every yard is different. Some cater to the yachtsman, others to working types—small fishermen and trawlers, still others to the ponderous bulk of tugs and barges, ferries and industrial craft. Myself, I like the small yard up a creek where the people seem to be in the business because of their love of working with their hands, creating a functional, practical thing of beauty and character that can take the seas, the load, the challenge of a harsh environment, yet remain in harmony with it. Warren Taylor was willing to take on the job of plugging the gaping holes in *Sylvia II*, and he had sufficient seasoned lumber in the loft of the boat shed. I'd suggested that he haul her and put her "on the hill" for the long job of restoration, so as not to tie up his railway. He disagreed: "Bob, an old boat like her really suffers out of water. Let's fix those holes and put her back overboard. Then you can work on her as you see fit." That made sense, and Craig Willis started the engine to let the cradle down.

As she came out of the water we began to get the good news. Though the worm-shoe was torn askew, the much-feared damage below the waterline consisted mostly of chafing. She had been built with natural knees, and not a one was broken. Everyone got to work right away, especially Mary, who put herself in charge of mud removal. She had no trouble getting started, for she could walk through the hole in the bow. She was scraping up mud and throwing it out that hole with a vengeance when she heard protests from the carpenters who were trying to replace the fractured planking. She withdrew peaceably and began throwing mud over the stern, which was where I was working. She said she never knew a charwoman to have so much trouble.

Carpenters quickly sawed out the shattered wood, staggered the butts and began replanking immediately, while I worked on the other most pressing problems. In three days *Sylvia II* was back in the water, with a new worm-shoe, fresh bottom paint and her hull whole again.

~~~~~~~~~~~~~~~~~~~~~~

In the search for good, sound wood to repair the damage to *Sylvia II*, I became interested in woods again. Where today can one find stout timber, heart of longleaf pine, white cedar (juniper, we call it down here), live oak? You may say, "That stuff is obsolete. Today we use steel, aluminum, fiberglass, miracle plastics for our boats." Yet wood is still the miracle material, and the cost to man is far less, for not only does it provide homes, boats, and heat; it supplies oxygen while it grows, shelters wildlife, slows floods, reduces erosion and protects from droughts, moderates climate and keeps deserts at bay, gives beauty, shade, and solace.

I'm still looking for an iron mine or an aluminum smelter that is not a blight on the land, a chemical factory free from obnoxious wastes and odors, fiberglass that does not remove a non-renewable resource. Recent news mentioned the clearcutting of 250-year-old trees in Oregon. Now I'm not opposed to cutting a tree, nor am I entirely against clearcuts, any more than I am against modern medicine. But, as in modern medicine, it's all in knowing how, where, and when to apply the treatment.

First, to gain perspective, a 250-year-old tree is to be treasured. It's older than our nation; it was living before the French and Indian Wars. Replaced today, it would be the year 2233 before the replacement could attain the same size and maturity. It's like melting down the Liberty Bell—they are so few and far between. Equally significant is that, though the South leads the nation in forestry, the far western forests, including those of Alaska, are being ravaged by timber-hungry money-grubbers intoning the magic phrase, "The Economy."

But is the wood being replaced? Timber companies' advertising says it is. They may be correct. But what is the replacement? Pulpwood. On National Forest and industrial timber lands, less than one tree in ten is a hardwood. Show me a case where public lands are being planted with white cedar, oak, walnut, pecan, or hickory, and I'll show you ten of slash pine that will be harvested like a field of corn by the time it gets to the diameter of a saucer. Then show me a house built of that kind of wood.

The forest products industry is heading for trouble in monoculture. Witness what happened to the residential monoculture of American elms: Dutch elm disease. Today the pine bark beetle is devastating vast timber areas. The beetle was a minor pest until the woods were filled with its special delight. Then it, too, began to multiply. Farmers—at least some of them—learned long ago about crop rotation. Timber interests claim to be farming trees. True; yet they seem to have missed a few lessons. Still, it's their land, and if this is the way they want to go, so be it. But when it comes to public land—and less than one-fifth of the nation's forests are under federal management—it's inexcusable. The public lands, including National Forests, belong to the people, not to a few timber companies. The argument is that public forests are being asked to produce more timber to keep prices from rising. This puts government in competition with private industry.

Most important, timber should be a by-product of our National Forests, as are water, grazing lands, recreation, and wildlife habitat. Our National Forests are the reserve. In World War II the wood for the famous PT boats came from an ancient forest whose logs lay buried in a sphagnum bog in New Jersey. Today it's very doubtful that, with possible exceptions in southern Alaska or some lost forest in Siberia or Brazil, this amount of wood could be found in sufficient quantity and quality to repeat such boat building. Fiberglass? It's based on oil. Steel? Our reserves are dwindling. Aluminum? One of the largest energy consumers in all industry. No, only through wise, long-term planning can our renewable resources be counted on, and most of that will be up to the small private landholder. As an average, an acre of woodland will produce, in continuing supply, a cord of wood a year. A cord can provide heat, shade, protection, and beauty, while still producing. Try to match it.

In the rest of the world, one-third of all wood consumed is used as firewood for cooking and heating. Today, because of increased demands, large areas of Africa and India are denuded, leaving swirling dust storms and growing deserts in their place. Today the manure that used to fertilize fields is the fuel, and the impoverished land becomes still less productive. America is the bread basket of the world, and our trees are a very important part of our abundance. We cannot afford the waste and the failure to replace. No matter how many times we might try to plant a fiberglass tree, I have yet to see one growing.

Well, we did find wood for deck and cabin repairs. The cabin sides had been constructed with double-planking of tongue-and-groove juniper. That was almost a thing of the past, but James Gillikin had some lying hidden in the back of a warehouse, and it proved to be of top quality. Soon *Sylvia II* was roughly closed in and protected from the weather. Inside the cabin, progress was slow but steady. First, there was light, with half-inch Plexiglas replacing broken portlights, new gaskets all around, and a skylight in the hatch cover. With a few quarts of degreasing fluid, and hours of scraping and sanding, the oil- and salt-beslimed overhead was stripped. We replaced missing floor boards and hatch covers, and Mary's efforts were beginning to show as buckets of old paint chips were toted ashore. Weather was the major deterrent to rapid progress. Dry and warm days could be spent on deck or other outside work, wet and windy days on the engine and interior finishing. March brings a period of "Old Quawk" weather, but we knew that with the coming of spring things would get better.

~~~~~~~~~~~~~~~~~

There's no sense in sitting around the fire waiting for spring to happen, though that's what we were doing when Franc White called to suggest a fly-in camping trip to Portsmouth Island, which lies about midway on the North Carolina coast between Capes Hatteras and Lookout. Charlie McNeill was maintaining the Henry Pigott house there and had offered us the use of it. It was a welcome opportunity.

Next day we were on the early ferry from Cedar Island to Ocracoke Island, across the inlet from Portsmouth. From the ferry landing at Ocracoke we drove to the general store to pick up a few last-minute items before going on to the small airstrip a few hundred yards from the village. On schedule, a zebra-striped light plane whistled in and taxied to where we were standing at the edge of the strip. Franc yelled from the cockpit, "Get in, Bob! You're next!" I'm nervous about these little planes, having spent too many hours in the air during a couple of wars to have faith in anything that doesn't flap its wings. I felt shoehorned into the tiny back seat of the Cub—at six feet two, I'm not exactly small. Franc comes in a somewhat larger size that filled the front seat. The little Lycoming engine, or whatever kind of egg beater it was, would have a job, I figured.

From previous experience I also knew that the short, grass-paved airstrip on Portsmouth Island had a sand trap in the middle. But it was too late. The engine was snarling and we had begun to roll. Mary stood by our gear looking anxious. I tried to turn my head for a last look, but there wasn't room. The plane lumbered a bit, the tail lifted, and the dunes raced by. So far, so good.

To our right, beyond the oldest lighthouse in Carolina, the harbor had a silver sheen and the village was taking shape. We rose higher, and to the left was broad Ocracoke Inlet, once one of the American Colonies' most important. Through this inlet came vital supplies to General Washington that enabled the American Revolution to succeed. At one time Ocracoke Inlet even surpassed New York in numbers of ships entered through customs. Below, blue and green waters mingled with yellow sands and fingerlike channels along the edges. This was Teach's Hole, where the most famous of all pirates, Blackbeard, met his fate. Surprised by a crew of the Royal Navy led by Lieutenant Maynard, he and his crew were overpowered and captured. Blackbeard's head was lopped off, and his bloody career as the scourge of the Carolinas and the Caribbean was ended.

There was scarcely time to think about all this history and at the same time watch the intricate channels, the small islands, and the obscure bars that make water navigation to Portsmouth today impossible except by very small boat. Now we were over a low, wide island that reached out of sight in a hazy horizon. A tiny cluster of buildings, half hidden in a small copse, was dominated by two buildings: a church, spired and white, standing lonely and almost defiant in a minute clearing; to the east of it the shake-sided buildings where the Life Saving Service once waited for distressed ships and seamen. Alongside was the airstrip, small enough to make a carrier pilot blink and take a wave-off.

Beyond, to the east, the everlasting sea that extended to the edges of the earth lapped at a barren, exposed beach nearly a mile wide. Just a few low dunes and an occasional clump of beach grasses marked the high tide line. The flats stretched out, beaten and storm-swept, as far as I could see to the sou'west, and back towards the inland ocean locally called Pamplico Sound. It was total isolation. Only the small pockets of green huddled on the island's backside stood above the reach of a normal storm. Among other things, I saw the tattered remains of a long-wrecked plane lying in the bushes.

Franc made a couple of passes and another circle before he throttled back, skimming the yaupons and salt-carved oaks. "Hang on!" He turned, sliding in a sideways skid, then chopped the throttle, and we thudded in, bouncing towards that soft, sandy center. A quick turn and the Cub lurched to a stop near his wife and their gear. I was sweating when I got out. I think Franc was too, but he immediately taxied to the far end, turned, raced the engine, and let loose the brakes. The zebra stripes rushed along, gaining speed, bounced over the hole and disappeared, sending a cloud of gulls swirling into the air behind us.

Looking around, I could see a few remnants of a concrete foundation. What looked like a well was all overgrown with brush. Beyond was the church spire. A worn brick roadway led in that direction. Nearby, the collapsing remains of a building were buried beneath vines and other growth. From behind me came the distant sound of winter surf and the mewing of gulls. It suddenly seemed very lonely.

It was a long time before I could hear the buzz of the plane again over the constant roar of the ocean. The zebra stripes raced in low and crabbed onto the field. Mary climbed out with our supplies, and I helped Franc screw the ground anchors into the sandy soil, snubbing the plane down tightly enough so that even a strong wind couldn't dislodge it. Picking up boxes and bags, we made for the small pink house that was snuggled among the bushes a quarter- to a half-mile away.

This house by Doctors Creek, a story and a half tall with front and back porches and woodburning stove, had been the home of one Henry Pigott, best known to old-timers as the mailman who poled out in a skiff to meet the mail boat that once ran between the fishing village of Atlantic and Ocracoke Island. He had passed on some years before, but his cottage had been kept just about the way he'd left it. Gutters caught rain water and drained it into a big tank back of the house. A small pitcher pump brought it into the kitchen. Near the back door a roofed, screened box, like a doll's house on pilings, served to keep food safe. Along with a few decoys, a litter of lumber, nails, glass, and all the items needed to keep things in repair on a very isolated island were sheltered in a small outbuilding. Close by on the shore lay an overturned skiff. Inside as outside, the house was neat and well maintained. The three rooms downstairs were small, those upstairs even smaller, pinched by the steep slope of the roof.

It was a typical cool, late winter evening. We built a fire in the stove and lit the oil lamp. Our wives prepared dinner over a propane stove while Franc and I made plans. He was filming a documentary. I hoped to get some stills. Everything was comfortable and snug, with good friends and good food—what more could we ask?

With the setting sun, the stillness of night had crept over the island, enveloping Doctors Creek. When I stepped out of the house there was no breeze to rustle the trees. There was no moon. The marshes were in deep black shadows. Scarcely noticed, a cloud had moved across the heavens, adding to the feeling of complete and absolute darkness. The lamp inside cast beams of yellowish light through the windows, only to be swallowed by the night. To the south, the low rumble of distant surf was an endless murmur. My eyes tried to adjust as I felt my way to the creek bank. I listened, and heard from a yaupon bush close by the sleepy chirping of small birds, disturbed by my presence or bickering over perch preferences. The cloud slid away like a stage curtain, revealing a few stars, then gradually disclosing a universe of glittering gems. Ink-black waters of the creek mirrored silvery images. Clumps of marsh grass were black on black.

A shooting star arched across the heavens. Out of the stillness a flock of Canada geese barked softly, to be echoed shortly by another flock, probably rafted somewhere on the sound, rocking comfortably in the safety of deep water. A thin cloud slipped across the sky, blotting out the stars. Far away on the horizon a light shone brighter than the others, Ocracoke Light, that had warned seamen of unseen dangers in the shoals for two centuries.

Yes, all was right with the world. Here, where there are few of the modern conveniences we're told are so essential, man finds that he can adapt quickly and easily. Electricity is missed little after the first day. It's not much harder to strike a match than to flip a switch. Television is soon forgotten. The plight of the world no longer seems real. Life readily becomes simplified: the flight of a heron has more significance than the ranting of a petty official. Here one does not have to inhale the stench of exhaust, witness the funeral pyre of a forest dying for the financial benefit of a real estate developer, nor see the earth torn asunder by clutching dragline or snorting bulldozer. It may be smug of me, but though I do appreciate that the elves of the Black Forest are busy building VWs and the Japanese building TVs, I'm glad I'm not completely tied to them. I can get along just fine on back roads without interstates, and I've enjoyed life without electricity. While I'm not denying their advantages, these conveniences do have drawbacks. In this case, I was grateful for the escape, and glad for the escape mechanisms.

Next morning we sat on the back porch to watch the sun rise. We could see the first light shining through the breakers, illuminating them with silver and gold undertones. At the proper time we made morning colors, so that the otters and owls on the island would know that someone was in residence at No. 1 Doctors Creek.

Portsmouth Village is thought of as a ghost town. True, no one resides there permanently any more, except in eternal rest behind the church, or in family plots about the island. And the homes, for the most part, are gradually decaying into the hummocks and marshes. Roofs have fallen in; graying shingles mouldering with green and silvery mosses are returning to the basic elements. But some of the homes whose windows vacantly reflect the red of evening sun are still neatly kept. Lawns are tended and flowers nod in the breeze even in midwinter. The tall church stands as it has for the past eighty-odd years, painted, neat, clean, waiting silently for a congregation that rarely comes except for occasional weddings and reunions.

It is a pleasure to walk a few miles along a lonely beach: no stoplights or beer cans, just waving grasses bowing to a brisk wind. A brilliantly clear winter sky, a warm sun reflecting off a rolling sea, a flight of pelicans gliding just above the water, following the troughs, rising and falling with the waves. A feather tumbles end-over-end down the beach. The senses sharpen, our ties with the natural world becoming more apparent. The ghost crab's sandy world is all-important to it, but no more significant to self than the sanderling's world, nor that of the raccoon on the sandbar gathering its supper. Anyone can see fool's gold. To the unobservant a gold mine is but a pile of rubble, rock and sand, but to discover the contents one must learn to observe and find the value hidden within the ore. Crush, pulverize, amalgamate, wash and manipulate—in this way you discover the value, the gold. You cannot sense your harmony with nature on a city sidewalk or in a room without windows.

The breakers are not far off. The island is nearly gone. Though it appears large on map or chart and from the air at low tide, in reality nothing more than those few small hummocks and marshes is above high water. Since early times, as elsewhere on Atlantic barrier islands, trees were cut to build homes, boats, ships, and fences. Maritime forests were cleared to plant crops and pasture livestock—often on open range—destroying stabilizing vegetation and ultimately permitting the sands to migrate ever faster. With each storm still more was lost, rendering the land less and less hospitable. Not until the late 1950s were the last cattle and horses removed from the Outer Banks, except for Shackleford.

The grass is returning to Portsmouth Island, and the trees also. Nature is working its long process of recovery. With the island now a historic site within Cape Lookout National Seashore, it should remain a monument to man's dreams and heroism as well as his greed and ignorance.

One could spend years living in peace on such an island, abandoned and isolated but for occasional surf fishermen and passing Park rangers. Portsmouth is cold and storm-swept by winter, hot and mosquito-infested by summer, but insulated from man's frantic world by miles of open sounds, dangerous shifting shoals and inlets, roadless beaches of soft sand. The fish boat passing offshore or the high-flying aircraft is a reminder that this is as close to a lost world as one can find today.

We oystered and filmed and explored the remnants of this almost-ghost town, one of the continent's earliest settlements. We were unable to find the site of the old Naval hospital that had boasted five hundred beds, nor the marble tombstone of one of the early governors. But somewhere beneath the brush, or perhaps sunk into the sea, are the footprints of a distant and nearly forgotten past.

After almost a week Franc packed up his film, and we untied the plane for the trip back to civilization. We drove up to the landing just as the ferry pulled away, but we didn't mind much: an overnight in

Ocracoke would ease the cultural shock of returning to the mainland. We walked sandy back streets, then checked into the Island Inn, a rambling hotel that seems to have retained the spirit of old Ocracoke. Clam chowder at dinner, fried country ham at breakfast, and the long ferry trip to Cedar Island allowed us to idle gradually into the faster pace that is trying to catch up even with life on Peltier Creek.

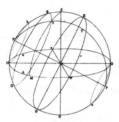

OLD QUAWK AND THE
IDES OF EQUALITY

*Nature's calendar is precise, based on the time that earth circles
the sun; thus the exact second of equinox and solstice can be
determined. Fishermen swear at and by the Ides of March.*

Long before the March 15 income tax deadline was advanced, or set back, depending on one's viewpoint—in
either case, a snare and a delusion—and probably even before
Julius Caesar got in trouble on account of the Ides of March,
assorted astrologers, Greeks, gypsies, and Carolina fishermen
have known that March is a month to stay close to home and
mind one's own business. And March 16 is an absolute don't-
leave-your-fireside day.

Contrary to the idea that traditions are being shattered
right and left, they are actually being reinforced all along.
Take, for example, an instance of a century or so back. A
nor'easter, one of those winter gales that habitually assail our

coast, carried onto the shores of North Carolina's Outer Banks a creature the local beachcombers called a "South American Indian," which was about as foreign a handle as they could give a man whose voice and language were totally strange to them.

He was a swarthy-visaged chap, wearing the long pigtail common to the sailors of the time, and he spoke in a manner the Bankers could compare only to the voice of the black-crowned night heron. That strange bird was called a quawk, a name approximating the guttural sound it gave in taking flight. Before long the bit of flotsam they'd picked up on the beach came to be called "Old Quawk," and he took up fishing with the natives, there being no bridges to the mainland in those days. It wasn't love, but lack of transportation, that placed early man on the Outer Banks.

Acquaintance proved the name appropriate, for the sailor of the dark countenance would rant and rave and curse something awful and was a real hardhead. There were as yet no squareheads on the Outer Banks. Come mid-March the wind can and does blow with near-hurricane force, bringing rain and storm and heavy seas. This is in order to give advance notice of what is known as the vernal equinox.

All sensible coastal residents know this, and knew it then. So when they found out that Old Quawk planned to go fishing on March 16, it being on Sunday besides, his friends, even though they didn't like him a whole lot, urged him not to go. They could see the storm clouds to the nor'east, and so could he, but he was so contrary that he just blasphemed and shook his fist at the storm and set sail anyhow. Now the night heron is a lone fisherman, too, doesn't fly with the rest of the seagoing fowl. As Old Quawk set sail into the teeth of the storm, a lone heron of the species from which the sailor had got his name took flight right behind him into that wall of wind and water. The strange call of man and bird was soon swallowed up in the storm and neither was ever seen again.

Coastal folk, native and non-native, like to brighten up an otherwise dull winter, and some years ago Carteret Country took to celebrating Old Quawk Day. All sorts of contests were to be held on the shores of Bogue Sound. One coastal native suggested that the weather could be expected to fit the occasion and that leaks in foul weather gear should be patched. Sure enough, the celebration was just getting underway when the sky darkened, the wind picked up, the ocean roared, and great sheets of rain lashed the assemblage, there to witness the Fisheries Commissioner's throwing out the first fish to open the season.

The storm was so fierce that it nearly blew the fish back in the Commissioner's face. Umbrellas turned inside out, speeches couldn't be heard in the gale, raincoats were ripped apart, picnic tables upset. The art show was blown off the seawall, the street dance had to be canceled, and utterances in the quawk-calling contest couldn't get out of the callers' throats or were carried out to sea without ever being heard. Then, as a testimony to contrariness, the winner of the title of stubbornest man in Carteret turned out to be a girl.

And now a new season has begun, the earth having swung complainingly once more past the spring equinox. Astronomers will tell you that the sun's declination has passed the equator. That's their story, and their privilege. I prefer to think of it as the time of year when spring is moving north at a rate averaging seventeen miles a day, when birds following the ice line move towards their ancestral breeding grounds. Some will settle on the tundra of the far north, where, in its brief ice-free period, they must raise their young to migration size.

Nighttime tells me, too, for in the darkness of the southwest sky the Belt of Orion seems dimmer, reflected still more palely in the smooth, black waters of the creek; the winter constellation of the hunter is soon to be hidden until its return to the cold eastern heavens next fall. It will be replaced by Scorpius, that cluster of stars found in midsummer along the southern horizon. I like to stand at creekside while the moon casts its misty glow over the sounds and watch the heavens move in a time and space far beyond the comprehension of man. It puts things in better perspective, for who can ponder the precision of the stars in their timeless, orderly movement and see man's mad pace as anything but a passing fad? The stars were the same for the Phoenicians, the Egyptians, the Chinese, and the aboriginals as they are for us today.

∽∽∽∽∽∽∽∽∽∽∽∽∽

The lifeblood is rising in the trees. In maple country the taps are dripping the watery sap that must be boiled and boiled until it becomes syrup. The sunrise is just about due east now. Instead of getting up late and sulking across the southern sky, the sun is getting bolder, and its warmth is penetrating the soggy earth, not just glancing off as it did all winter. Willow catkins and beach plum blossoms are out; dandelions are springing up in yards. Time for sulphur and molasses to thin the sluggish blood of winter, ward off the miasmas, and prepare one for spring. Hunting is over except for the spring turkey gobbler season, but the whelking season is on.

There aren't many true-hearted whelkers left nowadays—easy living, poor whiskey, and other signs of dwindling national morality have whittled away at the remaining numbers of us stalwarts. But, as inevitably as the migratory flight of the wild goose, the season has again rolled around for this unique pursuit. For those who have never gone a-whelking, a whelk is not like a nauga, which has only a hide. It's more like a big snail, and is referred to as a conch. My literal-minded wife says that they are not conchs, that conchs live in the tropics and up here they're whelks. Still, they look like snails, but that's not right, because Frenchmen eat snails; no self-respecting web-footed Carolinian would touch one. Instead, they eat whelks and call them conchs, and in spring the competition for them is as tough as the conchs are, which have all the tenderness of a truck tire.

Each spring we undertake a snail safari, and one year we were making preparations to go into the wilderness of mud flats where our quarry was known to hide out when I remembered that Franc White had always wanted to go on such an expedition. A back-up man would be good, I thought, so I called him. "Bring your Browning over-and-under, a good supply of No. 4 shot, and maybe that Irish setter of yours could point 'em. He's got a good nose. And bring your tenny runners. If you can move fast enough, we may be able to get you a few to film for your show." Franc has a TV outdoor show for which he dresses up in a bush jacket and proceeds to cook various things, when he doesn't have anything else to do. Well, he was on his way.

Selecting the only motor I had that would still run, I put it on the stern of the aluminum skiff. Franc and his dog followed us in our canoe, at the end of a tow line. We headed down the channel into the teeth of a nor'easter. With spray flying and wind howling, we bucked and rolled in heavy seas and plugged on. I could see that Franc was having trouble as another sea dolloped me in the face and Mary set to bailing. Across the foam he yelled, "Cast me off!" In Carteret County this means, "Tie me loose!" I complied amidst the spray, and Franc paddled on past us. I had the motor wide open, too. I hate showoffs who pass me in canoes. Someday, I figured, I'd have to clean the barnacles off the bottom of the skiff and put new spark plugs in the motor.

Whelks are hard to spot when only a knob protrudes, which explains why some of them are called knobbed whelks. We did find a half-dozen—considering that they weigh in at around a pound of meat each, enough for an appetizer. The late Euell Gibbons, who always enjoyed things that tasted like wild hickory nuts, wrote of them as large, edible gastropods that open clams and such by grabbing them with their feet. The whelk then frams the clam repeatedly against those knobs until the clam's shell breaks. Now I didn't know that, but it's a real good story.

To clean a conch is a right perplexing problem for a novice. The easy way is to take a large hammer, axe, hatchet, or maul and fracture the shell, then extract the remnants. But because women like these shells to set around for stumbling over and dusting, they usually want shell and meat separated without violence. So my practice is to throw the conchs in the freezer. When completely frozen, they're brought out to thaw. Then they'll slide out easily. The way some Florida conchs do it (I am here referring to *homo sapiens*, sub-species Florida Keys native) is to hang the conch by a fish hook inserted in the operculum. They claim that the steady weight of the shell on the muscle causes the animal to tire and lose its grip. All I can say is that when I tried that method, after a few days the stench was as strong as the muscle, forcing me to abandon the experiment. Perhaps Floridians prefer that stronger flavor. The vacated shells are esteemed as flower pots, and in pairs—left-handed and right-handed—they can become Bahama mittens, used by the islanders to prevent skinning the knuckles in a fight.

Conch or whelk meat is so tough, but so tasty, that I have designed a secret weapon for subduing it. I call it a conch zonker, a very long-handled live oak mallet with formidable teeth. After cutting the meat in quarter-inch slices, I beat them mercilessly, after which Mary sautés them tenderly. So the snail safari was a success, but, though Irish setters may point well on dove, quail, dimwits, and towhees, they aren't worth a darn for whelks. I couldn't hit one on the rise anyway.

〰〰〰〰〰〰〰〰〰〰〰〰

With only a thin crescent shining through scattered clouds, the moonlight across the water is a feeble blue. The wind, though light, is cold and damp. From a patch of woods to the west the tremulous query of an owl comes faintly, to be drowned out by dogs' barking. Then all is still, and the owl repeats its question. Clouds slide across the darkened face of the moon, now growing into the year's crow moon. On the northern plains it was so called because the crows were the first birds to stir, following the isotherms as they moved slowly northward, feeding on winter kills as snow and ice retreated. It was a sign of hope, for in the earth's eternal motion from season to season, the vernal equinox occurs during the crow moon. Like a symbol of the season, a crow had flown to the top of our lonesome pine this morning to watch me at work on the boat. You know, that crow has it made: nothing to do but fly around, keep an eye on things and make an occasional comment. And he owns that tree. Fact is, he owns the forests too, despite what the Forest Service, the Department of Agriculture, or the Secretary of the Interior may think. And he'll tell you so. What's more, he claims a good hunk of the whole world. If someone contests it, he'll be glad to fight, or share it, or skip the whole thing, depending on who challenges him. He's a right smart bird.

On the Carolina coast the crow moon might be called the cormorant moon, for this is also the time when those long-necked, ungainly black water birds begin to appear in numbers. One by one, then by the hundreds, waves of cormorants wing above a wind-tossed sound, a sou'wester picking up the water's chill and returning it to the north where it belongs. Fishermen, including Morehead City's Promise Landers, call these birds "Bogue Sound lawyers." Each bird in solemn black appears to have a cigar in its mouth. To others, this could be known as the skate moon, for now vast schools of skates and rays come in search of shellfish and other seafoods.

Crabs are emerging from their winter beds and beginning their quest for food. Jimmies are first, the she-crabs staying in deeper water for a bit longer. Landsmen find their promise of spring in the reappearance of the purple martin. Martins come from afar, traveling even greater distances than do seed catalogs. Leaves are pretty well out, and the southwest breeze, though not yet balmy, no longer carries a deep-freeze impact. Rushing the season are the fishermen, hanging over pier rails and boat rails, fishing and/or feeding the fish.

The fish are on the move, and the birds are on the wing, but one of the most spectacular migrations is that of the waterborne snowbirds. Big, luxurious floating palaces; sleek, powerful yachts and sportsfishermen; double-ended personality boats; sailboats of every design, motor sailers, and clunkers; all are making their way north now. Rich and poor, they start somewhere around Miami, follow "The Ditch" through Florida's Gold Coast, behind Cape Canaveral, hopeful of seeing a migrating space vehicle. On they come, into the swampy, twisting rivers of Georgia, where mudbanks meet the sea among the Golden Isles; through the abandoned rice fields and great sounds of the Carolinas they disappear to the north, some not stopping until they reach Canada and the Great Lakes. Being a snowbird is one of life's greatest luxuries, for a select few. Only the independently rich or the independently poor can afford to go this way.

The long black lines of Bogue Sound lawyers and the returning snowbirds stir my wanderlust blood almost as much as does the northward passage of geese, the epitome of limitless horizons and uncontrollable yearnings. To some folks a mere dandelion evokes these emotions, but surely no dandelion can have the impact of the nomads of the sky. I get to thinking of those still-unexplored places—the magic stream alive with trout somewhere in the Blue Ridge, where dogwoods bloom with the same abandon as the leaping fish, or a dark and moody lake dotted with pond lilies and full of sulking big bass—and I can't choose among them all. I miss the Everglades and the snook and the tarpon, and I want to hear again the snort of the curious mule deer back in the Grapevine Hills of west Texas, the burst of a pheasant from Dakota grasslands.

Yes, spring fever is a dangerous and easily contracted disease, for which there is no preventive medicine. It can be cured only by devotion to self and soul. It is the time when the storekeeper must hang on the door the sign "Gone Fishing"; when the legislator gazes out his window a little more listlessly than usual, no different from the schoolboy. This inevitable fight between duty and pleasure brings to mind the story of the fellow fishing by the roadside. He was casting into a bass bed when, in a vigorous back cast, the lure snagged the motor of an outboard heading west behind this car doing about—well, it seemed a lot more than fifty-five. Our friend set the hook and reared back, being a game fellow. Later he claimed he didn't have much choice; he'd hung on as best he could. When the line ran out, he'd tried to stand on it. I suspect the driver was bewildered when he found a plastic worm on thirty-five-pound mono attached to a speed stick. I once found a bottom rig attached to the mast of my boat. Guess I caught it passing under a bridge, but there was no fisherman attached—not even a rod.

Other folks, maybe more single-minded than I, have already repaired their fishing rods, replaced the loose guides, oiled the reels. But repair time for me gets completely out of hand from the moment I pick up the first broken rod. I get to puttering and dreaming of how it got broken in the canoe in the rapids of the Bitterroot River out in Montana. That leads to the possibility of ordering a new tip—except hasn't Montague quit making bamboo rods? Well, surely Orvis or Leonard still does, so out come the catalogs for comparison. This leads to graphite vs. fiberglass, though I'm not going to buy right now anyway. . . . By this time my wife issues chow call, which I've never been known to miss. So the rod joins the battered and honorable collection gathering dust in the corner.

Each rod, each gun is a story, a series of adventures and misadventures. Old companions, faithful and silent. There must be eighteen fishing rods hanging or sitting around, some broken or missing parts, but most just waiting for the moment, for salt or fresh, for bass, muskie, trout, or grayling; for amberjack, dolphin, king, or Spaniard; for pier, surf, or boat. I sure hope no one ever finds an inoculation against spring fever.

This morning, inspired by sun shining, flowers flowering and birds tweeting, I looked upon the old Sea Horse resting in the shade of the shop. It isn't that old, in terms of outdoor motors, but everything over a year old seems to be viewed as venerable, and all things that I have are considerably venerable. At least they act that way. With all the modern technology of superior metals and machining, of micrometers and kilometers, these machines have become "ultra-sophisticated," whatever that means, but I've never had one I'd trust an oar's length from the dock. I hung the motor on the rain barrel, and filled the tank. Then, the rewind mechanism having disappeared or expired long ago, I took a few turns with the starter cord and gave a yank. Then another, and another, until, hands raw and shoulder aching, I picked up the tools and put them away.

No one can kid me about outdoor motors. Just like other horses, they know when you are afraid of them and respond accordingly. That infernal machine understands that you don't understand and takes fiendish delight—you see, it really is ultra-sophisticated—in being perverse. As with an unruly animal, sometimes you've got to find someone who can train it properly. My Sea Horse is now being trained by mechanics at Boats, Inc. I hope they use a big whip. Outboard motorboats spell trouble in other ways. If you own one, the problems grow beyond the wildest imaginings. The feeding, at a buck and a half a gallon, is no sweat, especially when they won't consume. It's the dockage, the caretakers, the rusting trailers, the boatshed, the insurance, and, worst of all, the law.

31

If you own an outboard, you are law bait. There is forever the beady-eyed lawman, ignoring poachers and other villains, just waiting behind a channel marker to find an irregularity. On the other side of the coin, I guess I can't blame him. A recent survey showed that the most dangerous occupation of all, besides tree topping and walking city streets at night, is being a game warden. As a sheriff and a highway patrolman were discussing the hazards of their trade, they agreed that only a danged fool or a game warden would venture alone into the wild back country in search of an armed law breaker. Maybe that's the reason so many game wardens can be seen in boats, skulking behind nun buoys, rather than in the swamps: dedication can go only so far.

～～～～～～～～～～～～～～～～～

About the same time that conchs are surfacing, shad are beginning to run up the rivers. Mallards homestead nesting sites along the shorelines, birds warm up their courting songs—the love-smitten mourning dove's lonesome call is always earliest—and beach plum blossoms confirm man's hopes. University of North Carolina botanists base spring on when the average dogwoods, redbuds, and red maples come into bloom. While we prefer to judge by when the ducks get down to serious nesting, others go by the purple martins' arrival. The first purple martin scout has already surveyed the scene here, and a quick duck egg count in the briars and brambles above the tideline totals fifty-six. I'd say that it's serious and that certain precautions are in order.

First, get the outdoor motor back from the repair shop. Same story every year: wait until the last minute. Go through the tackle box to see if there are any shad darts left. There aren't, of course. Next, look over the skiff. Needs a few rivets. Bottom's worn down, and that dent on the gunnel is from a hurricane away back, when the skiff was blown against a tree. Glad we'd put out the anchor. The scratches and scars are honorable, from at least twenty-five years of hard use.

It was in Florida that the skiff was delivered to us at the marina. The truck drove up, and a big husky called to my wife and asked where to put it. She asked him to bring it down the pier to the boat. He ventured that it was too heavy and he'd have to leave it lying on the roadside. Mary told him, All right, leave it there and she'd take it down herself. He delivered it to the boat. The miles of lakes and rivers that tin skiff has explored, the hundreds of sandy beaches it has nosed onto, the oyster flats and mud banks, the duck hunting trips and swamp browsing, the hundreds of fish that have been caught from it, the dozens of logs it has been dragged across, the salt and spray, the hurricanes, the hours of blissful, lazy pleasure! Maybe I should set it up on blocks and retire it. The rugged little twelve-footer has worn out three motors and gone through several sets of oars, lost or stolen, and eight or ten anchor lines. But when I think of how much more life is left in that battered shell, I know we'll use it up and wear it out as tender for *Sylvia II*, if only Mary will remember to get some more rivets.

∞∞∞∞∞∞∞∞∞∞∞∞∞

When the wind is light sou'west across the sound, carrying the sweet scent of salt mingled with traces of sun-baked marshes, when an occasional white-topped cloud drifts overhead and a flight of skimmers is cutting through the water, it is tempting to abandon all plans and go sit on my favorite island and watch birds, or try the hammock slung between two live oaks. But I have a higher goal, which Mary refers to as that hole into which I steadfastly pour not only a great deal of time, but worse yet, money. I try to tell her that if she questions the financial aspects of boating she has no business even discussing the subject.

So much for my paraphrasing of J. P. Morgan. What it boils down to is that I have been left with only one assistant in the gradual restoration of the last of the old-time party boats. What was once enthusiastic cooperation has dwindled to a small green heron that keeps me company. Sitting on the bow line, it observes and makes suitable comments on my carpentry while watching for the passage of inattentive fish. It sees as its duty the thinning of the minnow population, thereby preventing overgrazing and possible starvation due to overcrowding of minnow habitat.

A lesson learned long years before had to be relearned: that this boat business isn't all it's cracked up to be; specifically, that one problem leads to another, to another, to another. As I mentioned at the outset, it had started with a simple hole through the side of *Sylvia II*, which caused a leak, which caused the boat to sink, in turn causing the engine and other equipment to fill with salt water. "Patch the hole!" you say. "Pump it out!" A lot you know about it—this only leads on to decks, to cabintops, to prop shafts, to fuel tanks.

Oh yes, those fuel tanks. Even Cap'n Theodore's troubles were not over after he'd sold the boat. The U.S. Postal Service, obliging and indiscriminate purveyor of good and bad tidings, delivered him a letter from the Coast Guard suggesting a $5,000 fine for having allowed the fuel and oil to spill from the engine and tanks when *Sylvia II* sank. His reported response: "Take me away! Lock me up! At least you'll have to feed me!" Well, it turned out to be one of those literal translations of pollution laws written for superships like *Torrey Canyon*, that weren't exactly meant for small boats sunk by hurricanes. Still, the moral seems to be: drain the gas and oil from your boat before sinking, and heaven help you if you spill any.

The original tanks had begun life as hot water tanks and were sadly rusted, but an abandoned fiberglassed metal tank and a much-too-large used fiberglass tank were available in the boatyard for twenty bucks. Craig Willis cut four feet off the end of the oversized one and refiberglassed it. Tested with a four-foot head of water, it proved satisfactory, and we installed the two tanks on deck, with benches over them. I put fill pipes on the outer deck, bringing them up to safety standards (previously the tanks had been filled inside the cockpit). Secured in chocks and strapped down under fixed benches, they could be inspected easily, and any flaw that should develop would be obvious. In the old days the fuel supply of these boats usually was a fifty-five-gallon drum lashed in the cockpit. The present capacity nears a hundred gallons, enough to run her for several days. We often cruise three long days without refueling and could probably do six before even beginning to look for a fuel stop.

Afloat was a long way from running. In the middle of the cabin sat the Chrysler Crown engine. It was a mess, though first aid had been administered in the form of washing and flushing with kerosene and oil. Now we pulled head, starter, generator, and distributor and checked them. A thorough soaking and washing in hot soapy water, I found, could be done at a self-service car wash. After a clear water rinse Mary baked the parts in the Shipmate oven at 150°. She gave the same treatment to the radio, but at 125° after the plastic microphone began to distort. A repairman checked the radio for ten dollars, and it has worked ever since. Generator and starter hadn't suffered from immersion, but the bearings were bad. I'd been told that Theodore started the engine with a hammer, but later I determined that it was because of a sticky solenoid.

We hadn't yet run out of engine problems. Fresh water cooled, with a dry exhaust, the old Crown had a cracked water jacket, but the cylinders were okay. The exhaust manifold was split lengthwise— at some time there had been a cold snap and no antifreeze. Scraping at the block and manifold with a file, I cleaned cracks as best I could, forced in Devcon and smoothed it, effectively sealing all leaks; later we had it welded.

Oil leaks were another problem: the prop shaft seal was shot, but my neighbor Joe Barbour, a master machinist, took care of it handily. By now we had received a parts and maintenance manual from the archives of Chrysler and located some oil seals. Next in order was a water pump: the original no longer had any impellers to speak of. For a hundred or so I could buy a replacement Jabsco, but this was out of financial reason. Behind Atlantis Marine—the name had a special significance somehow—a junked Crown, rusted and busted, had reasonably good water pump impellers, which I managed to obtain after a great deal of persuasion with wrench, hammer, and chisel.

We were stymied when it came to finding a voltage regulator. Most parts could be found in auto supply stores, but this electrical puzzle was to vex us for almost a year until I got smart, lifted the brushes to prevent drag and disconnected the wiring. Interrelated, generator and water pump could not be completely abandoned. I found a rebuilt alternator, hooked it up to a pulley off the flywheel— and no more problems.

I'd stripped the carburetor and cleaned it as well as I could. One battery, flushed and refilled with fresh acid, took a charge. The engine turned easily by hand now, and things were looking up until I tried to solve puzzles of timing and wiring. John Wyatt, a war surplus destroyer skipper, came by with his son Clinton to socialize and saw a challenge to their mechanical skills. With their help I could see that before very long *Sylvia II* would be cutting capers again.

After more than a month of repairs, and before a sailing date was in sight, I had dreamed up a way of defraying expenses, which I calculated would put me back in the good graces of my wife. By day, *Sylvia II* would be an old-fashioned party boat, equipped with a couple of crab pots, two or three clam rakes, a hank of net and a cook stove. And, oh yes, a rod and reel or so. She'd operate on the basis that boating is fun. She'd be for charter by the tide. On high tide we'd set a net and on low tide dig clams, as soon as I could work out a deal with a local clam hatchery for transplants. She'd likely sail no farther than the inlet, but make exploratory inland cruises.

Imagine, if you will, this trim vessel riding at anchor behind Shackleford Banks. After a lunch of bluefish so fresh they curl up in the frypan, we'd go on a clamming foray—perhaps even try to outrun a few crabs with a dip net. Swimming would just come naturally, and skindiving for drink cans ought to be real good. Ideally, one of the customers would be able to cook; otherwise, I'd have to hire a mate.

But the after-dark package would be best! At night I'd put a green felt-covered table over the engine, set up the *pachinko* (that's Japanese for pinball machine) and lay out a deck of cards. I could visualize it all: clustered in the darkened cabin under the glare of the engine room light hazy from cigar smoke lounge a crowd of men, stacks of poker chips, *pachinko* clanking and ringing bells. A real gambling ship! When summer folks went out for an evening cruise, they'd see this sneaky-looking, blacked-out ship pass in the night and hear the muffled sounds of a pinball machine and the slap of cards on felt. They'd know right off that it was no weed runner but the legendary gambling ship of Bogue Sound. There might be minor legal technicalities, but these could be solved easily by cutting the legislators in on the action.

WHEN FISH AND BUGS BEGIN TO BITE

All this dreaming wasn't getting the job done. We needed new dock space for *Sylvia*. The boatyard had a limited amount of room for working, and now that the major wood-working was finished she was taking up valuable space. Dockage is a growing problem along the coast. Waterfront-age is limited and expensive. Covered storage costs from seventy-five to several hundred dollars a month. Even an open slip starts at thirty, and ten dollars per foot per month is commonplace. It was now time to put up our own dock. Checking costs, I found that the best a contractor would do was twenty-five hundred to three thousand dollars. For my three-hundred-dollar boat!

Luck was needed, and it drifted in one morning. A tug-boat had sideswiped a channel marker on the Intracoastal Waterway, and the marker came bobbing into the creek

nearly submerged. The Coast Guard arrived promptly to remove it, and we offered a beach on which to abandon it. Heavily creosoted, twenty-five feet long and fifteen inches in diameter, it was the ideal start for a dock. Letters to the Coastal Resources Commission and the Corps of Engineers brought construction permits in short order.

Chopping one end of the piling to a point, my brother Bill and I rigged a series of blocks and tackle to trees nearby, planted two anchors on the offshore side, and began to sink this first piling. Extremely heavy, such a piling could not be lifted even by a muscle man. Bill and Mary operated a "come-along" winch while I put on waders to stand on one end of the piling and start it into the mud. Anchored guy ropes kept the top from swinging to the side. We worked at low tide, using a pump and garden hose to jet the piling about eight feet deep, which left twelve to fourteen feet for attaching the dock. We located two more scrap pilings, which we cut into shorter lengths and connected with timbers and decking from an old fish house that was being demolished. Total cost of materials was thirty-eight dollars in nuts, bolts, and nails, plus ten dollars for the permit. Counting many interruptions and high tides, it took us a week to build a triangular dock twenty by eight feet at its widest.

The new home for *Sylvia* was barely completed before the eviction notice became final. Just in time, too, for it was now the season when fish and bugs begin to bite. There is no rule that says both must bite at the same time, but they usually do. Sea mullet (whiting) are moving along the beach. Sea mullet are not exactly famous, yet the first spring run brings out the ocean pier fishermen to catch them two at a time, and only the uninitiated will say that it is not the most succulent saltwater fish. Then the predator species, like blues and king mackerel, will appear in the wake of their favorite food, fishes such as shad, jumping mullet, and menhaden. As for the bugs, the first one is the fishing bug, often called spring fever, followed by the bite of the wander bug, which becomes more frequent later in the season. Many insects are still in spring training, but their scouts are out.

Perhaps fishing is repugnant to some folks: stinking, slimy fish, a waste of time, an excuse for idleness. I can only refer to the movie cowboy who used to kiss his horse rather than the girl: there's no accounting for taste. In my opinion, fishing is one of the noblest of occupations, and this view puts me in the company of a lot of first-class folks. Let's begin with some bona fide fishermen-heroes, such as the one who liked fishermen so much that he walked across the water to help them. Further, St. Peter was a fisherman, and his muddy fingerprints are on our favorite panfish to this day; so say the Scandinavians, who long ago gave the name "Peter fish" to what is known to us as the spot. It makes one wonder how the red drum got the spot on its tail—was it the one that got away? That, too, may be the origin of fish stories, for the red drum is unquestionably a big fish.

Moving to more modern times, John Dillinger and Pretty Boy Floyd liked to go fishing, which explains why I didn't say that all fishermen are first class. But it did give them something in common with their archenemy, J. Edgar Hoover. Both of the Hoovers, especially the President, enjoyed fishing, as did FDR. Fishing is a great leveler, putting everyone on a common plane, although Mr. Hoover doubtless thought he had as much in common with the Public Enemies as he'd ever want. Among the great inventors, what was Newton really doing when he invented gravity? (There are those who insist it was a discovery, not an invention.) He was fishing. Why else would he be sitting under an apple tree thinking?

It is simple fact that non-fishermen aren't as thoughtful as anglers. Consider the word "angling"—it means thinking of new angles, which indicates that the fisherman is a profound thinker. Seriously now, most folks spend their lives racing around the way they drive cars—too fast. The only fishermen who do this are bass masters, but they're a relatively new breed and therefore one should not be too critical. They just haven't learned yet. Mark my word, the day will come when they, too, will develop into great philosophers.

Fishing was meant for nature lovers, philosophers, and people in need of a vacation. John Smith, while on a long vacation from England, was one of our first tourists. His comments indicate he may also have been a Chamber of Commerce founder, writing as he did that there is no greater satisfaction than "fishing for sport with hooke and lyne."

The foregoing comments were prompted by a go-getter who said that fishing is for dropouts, hippies, and such as that. Remarks of this kind raise my hackles, sparse gray ones. The types referred to are the very ones who don't try to outwit the finny tribe, because it takes concentration, endurance, determination, and more to make angling a success. And success, in contrast to the rest of the materialistic world, is not measured in pounds of fish.

Sportsfishing success is measured more by what one sees, feels, hears, and otherwise senses. A surf fisherman derives as much pleasure from watching the ocean waves roll ashore in foaming crescendoes, feeling the power of the seas pulling at his waders and undermining his footing on the beach, hearing the gulls cry and sensing the unending immensity of the ocean as he ever gets from snatching a flounder out of its favorite haunts. In bass pond or at streamside one is reminded of the interlocking of all natural systems, the insect, the snake, the frog, the bird, and the bass, and how they are related to the purity of water, the shelter of a tree, and how man fits. The catching of the fish is the frosting on the cake.

Man cannot remain arrogant or sustain false pride if he spends much time delving into the natural world. We can brag of our technology, of sending a man to the moon, but nature "invented" both. We can speak of our atomic power, but nature dumps more energy on the earth in a summer thunderstorm than does any explosion. There is only one force that has more effect on man, and that's woman—which is only natural, too.

∽∾∽∾∽∾∽∾∽∾∽∾∽∾∽∾

Spring is an accomplished fact now. It became more evident to us last night when Mary and I went out in the sound to check the gill net. It was late, and the world was shrouded in the blue-blacks of night. Only the flickering of far-distant lights reflected off the wind-rippled sound. Leaning into the oars, I felt the skiff skitter over the water, listened to the creak of wood in the row locks, the swish and gurgle of water past the thin, cold aluminum hull. I paused, oars dripping, so that we could look at the stars, unsullied by loom of shore lights, not obscured by blackness of riverbank and trees. The handle of the Big Dipper pointed towards the east. Spica and Arcturus were well above the horizon, and the Belt of Orion had already faded in the west. Sirius and Betelgeux were descending, sure signs of spring well established.

The damp warmth of a light southerly breeze might fool one, or the still-chilly waters penetrating the hull of the skiff might mislead, but there is no fooling the heavens. Even the sea birds, disturbed on a sandy shoal and muttering sleepily, were secure in their sensing the imminent return of fresh marine life for summer fare. Far to the south the surf collapsed softly on the strand, no longer the thunderous roar of winter storm that had dominated the past months.

This is the time of the return of green grass, so important to wildlife. And while the Banker ponies, scrawny and scruffy from a hard winter, are competing for the succulent green, winter snows are rushing downstream in a headlong race for the oceans, flooding forests and fields to sogginess, recharging swamps for the long, hot dry summer to follow. No matter what man does or commands, the winds, the rains, the snows, the heat of the sun will prevail.

We had picked up the net and returned to the creek before noticing the smell of oil. The water had seemed slick in spots; not much, just a thin film. But as I rowed through the blackness, past channel markers, over the shoal, around the breakwater and into the gloom of tall trees where a dim light marked our little pier, the thought persisted: what is to be coastal Carolina's future?

Our leaders in their infinite wisdom have declared us to be poor, downtrodden serfs, but they will save us from the distress of poverty. Their solutions, which we hear rattling in the wind, are industry and energy. But I see them as the Great Resource Exploitation and Expediting Department, offering us super tankers, super ports, super refineries, and vast petrochemical installations; super farms and phosphate mines, already proved to be super; atomic power plants—super, of course—offshore and on every river; pipelines and sulphuric acid and phosphoric acid plants, also super.

Meanwhile, they are begging the Federal government to give more of our money to paving and road building because of some emergency, and to be sure not to forget the poor, depressed housing trade so that we can strip more of our overcut woodlands to build condominiums for the poor on our about-to-be-paved-to–extinction barrier beaches. So we are to be saved with the very things that smothered such coastal states as New Jersey and others to the northeast. We will have a utopia of belching smoke, overcrowding, flooding sewers, bumper-to-bumper traffic, factory stench, fouled water, and—when the bubble breaks—long lines of unemployed. This, mind you, is so we won't have to suffer from the sweet smell of a magnolia, or have a place to sling a hammock. It will relieve us of the problems of ospreys and bluebirds by replacing them with wharf rats and garbage cans.

It's just that my idea of progress is somewhat different: progress doesn't have to mean giving up all that was desirable in the past. I see it as still including salty-sweet oysters that can be eaten where you find them, and deep woods and tall trees and good lumber and good books. I see progress as air fresh enough to be breathed deep, as more time for man to drift on a stream where he can catch fish, or as unpolluted beaches with a semblance of privacy for sitting under a sun filtered only by sunburn lotion, with room for a surf rod or a surfboard. I see progress as living in a place where your neighbors are good enough to be your friends and where, if you want, you can have a collard patch and a few sweet potatoes to go along with the oysters.

The basic problem is that we are still sidestepping the real issue. On the Statue of Liberty is inscribed, "Give me your tired, your poor, Your huddled masses yearning to breathe free, The wretched refuse of your teeming shore, Send these, the homeless, tempest-tossed, to me; I lift my lamp beside the golden door." But we've let the lamp get smoky and the door become tarnished. It was the same then as now—overpopulation of a world of finite resources. Conservation can only be a delaying tactic, a braking power. Development and consumptive use are necessary, but they lay down a racecourse, a speed-way, to ever-growing shortages. There is no panacea. Importing more energy only puts off the inevitable collision between what we must have to survive and who will be the survivors. The answer is as old as the dinosaurs: when the supply ends, so does the consumer. That's the ultimate in population control. First, man designed the candle to light his way; soon he found it not enough, so he lit both ends; now he's trying to burn it in the middle, too.

~~~~~~~~~~~~~~~~~~~~

Early mornings in spring are always beautiful in the tidal marshes and juncus sloughs, where all is mist-shrouded, and the rigging of small shrimpers jutting above the grasses marks the twisting course of the narrow channels. In front yards upturned skiffs, heaps of ghostly monofilament nets, and jumbles of crab pots further testify to the communities' strong ties with the sea. Splashes of yellow mark collard patches going to seed, and golden garlands of yellow jessa-mine herald spring from the treetops.

On such a morning we were out, having been summoned at an un-reasonable hour by one John Gaskill, to go longhauling. Far up the Merrimon Road we turned off the blacktop onto gravel, crossed a small bridge, and picked up a sandy trail that wound through the woods to end at a fish house. John was impatiently pacing the deck of a vintage Carolina fisherman rebuilt into a run boat. Grabbing cameras and jacket, I followed Mary aboard.

Lines cast off, old Gray diesel hammering belowdecks, *Robert King* slid between a pair of fish stakes and followed Jonaquin Creek to where it joins the Intracoastal Waterway. Before us the creek was mirror-calm, presenting nearly perfect reflections of a dark green shrimper lying against a dock, its image beginning to waver, and of moss-hung trees, weathered fish houses, and small homes. Skiffs and workboats lay on the beach in the clean untidiness of the fishing world. Laughing gulls, sparkling white and black, flew high, scouting, then dropped to follow our wake as we passed a range marker. The creek was wider now. Grassy banks and overhanging trees had given way to abrupt dredged cuts and raw banks. A single fisherman in a small boat waved as we entered the Neuse River, big and wide.

Leaving the channel, we cut across the edge of Garbacon Shoals. A hazy sun was hiding behind gray clouds while a nor'east wind was rolling small whitecaps down our way from somewhere around Cape Hatteras. The boat bobbed and twisted, knifing through the waves; Mary cooked breakfast, trying to keep the coffee pot from joining the sausage and eggs. A flight of coots high-stepped across the water, attempting to gain air speed before diving through a wave. In the distance a tug towing two barges was barely visible on the horizon. Turnagain Bay was on our starboard. We plunged on.

Now a run boat doesn't fish, it runs, to and from the fishermen, picking up their catches and running the fresh catch, iced down, back to the fish house for processing. And the fishermen won't tell you where they are fishing, because if they do, and get a good catch, sure enough, a whole passel of other fishermen will join and smother the area. Yet, ever since the invention of radio, fishermen have had to talk and brag. Maybe this is where the fisherman's reputation for tale-telling was developed. If you can't let others know of your catch, how can you brag? So codes are worked out, understatements and just plain exaggerations.

Listening to crackling, blasting radios above the whistle and thumping of a diesel, only an expert can manage to decode what is being said. From the unpainted beams overhead, the tiny radio's light glowed like a red eye as the speaker blared into John's ear. He leaned towards me and kept repeating above the engine noise, "Make a man deaf, you know . . . make a man deaf. . . ." My ears numb, I nodded, and John cranked up the volume another notch. Our rendezvous was behind a point of land, a shallow bay where two thirty- to forty-foot boats were straining, one at each end of a long net, as if in a giant tug-of-war. Called a long haul, seventeen hundred yards of net were stretched between the boats, closing a great circle near where we waited in the shallow lee of the marsh. The boats labored to close the gap, then smaller boats were poled to take up and reduce the circle, concentrating the catch.

44

In the commercial fishing world, all men work standing. Nets are pulled while the men stand in a boat or on a beach. And boats are poled mostly, not rowed. Only when work is over does anyone sit. The fishermen, wearing waders and foul weather jackets, were dropping overboard in chest-deep, chilly waters to work, the sun weakly illuminating the scene but the light north wind deepening the chill. Unlike trawling or beach seining, this kind of fishing is done without birds to cheer the fishermen. Occasionally a gull passed over. High overhead, jets blew by in blowtorch rumbles to pirouette in rocket runs over a distant target range. *Robert King* rolled in the slight swell. The stoutness, the simple efficiency and beauty of the round-sterned, straight-stemmed Carolina fishing boat, similar to our *Sylvia II*, is perfection in boat design. With shallow draft and fast displacement hull, it was built to take short mean seas, from either end. It has never been excelled. A distant kin resides in the Chesapeake.

The net was closing noticeably. John pulled the run boat alongside the work skiff where the net was being held, lowered a big basket by boom, and opened the hatches. Fishermen snatched sting rays and other undesirables from the catch as the load tumbled into the hold. Bluefish ran three-quarters to a pound, but one must have weighed fifteen to twenty pounds. Trout were a half to two pounds, though some were long as a man's leg, maybe fifteen pounds. There were a few flounder, jumping mullet, needle and hound fish, a glowering toadfish, a diamondback terrapin. The catch was duly iced as the netmen selected a few choice fish for themselves, loaded the rest of the net aboard the skiff, and left us. We dropped hatch covers in place, secured them and cleaned our lunch underway. The aggressive bluefish that I chose promptly sank its teeth like a bulldog into my pinky. Had it been the big blue, I'd be known today as Four-finger Simpson.

Mary cooked the fish crisp in very hot lard loaded with salt. A blue cloud filled the little deckhouse. Boiling coffee added its fragrance as we hurried home with a catch that wouldn't pay the expenses of the trip, much less help feed families or pay for boats and nets. Pushing on past Oriental and South River, we sucked on the last remaining morsels. John asked how I liked it. "Fine," I answered, "except I like my fish fresh," and continued picking my teeth with a bone. "The only way you'd get it fresher would be to get o'erboard and eat 'em outa the net," John grumbled, and swung back into Jonaquin Creek.

~~~~~~~~~~~~~~~~~~~~~~~~~~

Every evening, beginning in late spring, somewhere between afternoon coffee break and supper time, a long stream of boats swings bows to the north'ard, drawn towards Beaufort Inlet as if by a giant magnet. Like white butterflies on a shining sea of blues and greens, they assemble after gathering the nectar of the blue waters, rolling, dipping, bobbing, some darting along like swallows, scarcely skimming the surface. Others slowly and reluctantly leave the crashing breakers of the Cape Shoals where the bluefish and Spaniards roam. Still others come from the distant Gulf Stream drift lines where great marlin and sharks stalk their prey. They gather in a steady parade past the sea buoy and up the long channel. A few peel off near the Cape to follow the shoal, tortuous route to Harkers Island, but most file past the gray concrete and steel warehouses of the state's port. A few more drop off to take the inside channels to Bogue Banks, but the majority—comprising one of the finest sportsfishing fleets on the east coast—assembles along a quarter-mile stretch of the Morehead City waterfront.

One by one these charter sportsfishermen back into their slips to discharge passengers and cargoes of prize fish, from albacore and amberjack to tuna and wahoo, plus other favorites like marlin and mackeral. Actually, more than 350 species are caught from these rich waters, of which twenty-odd are especially prized as sports fish. Statistics tell us that crews with accumulated experience of well over six hundred years carry an average of twenty-eight thousand fishermen more than forty thousand miles to catch in excess of 350 tons of fish. It's cheaper, though, to buy them at one of the seafood markets along the waterfront, or eat a seafood special of broiled flounder at one of the sparkling restaurants perched over the water.

So what is the lure? It's that every day at sea is an adventure. It's the privilege of being offshore, out of sight of land or man's works, watching the sun rising from the ocean. To begin with, its golden rays reflect off the clouds as the light grows and the stars have disappeared. A pearl-pink sky fades with the first glittering shafts of light bouncing off a dark and mysterious sea. Then there's the serenity of a good boat slicing its steadfast way through a light swell, the freshening of the morning breeze when the sun finally lifts itself above the horizon. The black waters lighten to a deep blue, yet close about the water is so clear that one feels in suspension.

Next comes the attaching of baits and the slow trolling with outriggers bobbing in the rhythmic roll. Another vessel comes into view, and the radio crackles and fries with talk. A freighter on the horizon is a different world. Gulls mew and cry, following the wake hopefully, and then it's "Fish on!" The reel screams as line is sucked into the depths. Fishermen scramble, and there is desperate cranking and yanking. The rod dips and the fish fights for survival.

Line paying overboard screeches, other fishermen shout advice and encouragement, a blue-green flash reveals the fish rising in a wave, and the angler sees his prize for the first time. Wrist and arm strain. He pumps to recover line. Then the mate leans overside to make a sweep with the gaff. A kaleidoscope of color is the fish snatched aboard and flung, flapping and gasping, into the recesses of the fish box. Perhaps there is a momentary pang of sympathy for the already-fading catch, but it is soon forgotten, for another fish is on.

The skipper, a cheerful man with sunburned grin, watches from his aerie on the bridge, a sanctuary forbidden to ordinary mortals. Snow-white clouds on the horizon, blue sky against silver-blue sea, wind rattling in the rigging and the clatter of gear when the boat dives into a rolling sea, flashes of white caps on green and blue crystal. Boxes of fried chicken and boiled eggs are opened—some of the party have given up fishing early. The glare of a white-hot sun on the deck, the sea reflecting from every angle, the sun-and-wind-burned feeling growing as fish after fish goes into the dark, ice-filled box, to flap only a moment or two. Then a tall, black-bottomed cloud with slanting sheets of rain clatters across the sea, and the ocean sizzles in the white mist of water against water.

The day ends as choppy seas become the calm of the sounds, where crowds are waiting beneath flapping, snapping plastic flags at dockside. Fickle vacationers move from boat to boat while lines are secured and rumbling diesels quieted. Fish are thrown on the dock under the cleansing spray from a hose. Perhaps a picture or two follows, then the settling of the charter fee, the icing and packing of the catch, handshakes with the bronzed crew, and promises of return. The party heads for a seafood dinner and the crew turns to cleaning and refurbishing the boat to greet the next sunrise with a new party. Few skippers would trade this rugged, underpaid way of life for any other form of work. Only when the ravages of time and arthritis have taken their toll does the charterboat quit answering the siren call of the sea.

<hr />

Ocean voyages are supposed to be good for health and morale. Mary's idea of an ocean voyage is to be able to see the next anchorage as soon as she has left the previous one. Unfortunately, she suffers from motion sickness on any vehicle or vessel except a horse. Unfortunately for me, she never hesitates to recommend that I take an ocean voyage. Also, she has a co-conspirator, Gene Huntsman, who invites her to go on some junket and then settles for me—or should I say she sets me up, and the first I know about it is when she hands me my gear and says, "Have a good time!"

There was one time, though, when I got the call direct. It was like a dream come true, or maybe like winning the sweepstakes, when a voice drawled, "How'd you like to go on an all-expense-paid, five-day fishing vacation? Good meals, bunk, and all you need. We'll even furnish the tackle." What could I do but leap at this chance of a lifetime? Several days later I began to recall how the crimps for old whaling ships recruited crews: "All-expense cruise halfway around the world." Nagging doubt set in when Mary suggested that maybe

I should carry a bit of seasick medicine just in case. Suddenly it struck me that I really do get seasick. This cruise was to be an exploration of the reef fish populations, and the reefs are most common a long way offshore. I tried to convince myself that it couldn't be too bad.

So, armed with plenty of pills and other medicines, I put in my appearance dockside at the designated 1400 hours to meet the expedition leader. We weren't to leave until 1900 hours. The early mustering hour was so that we could tote those barges and lift those bales or whatever all that gear was heaped on the foredeck of the R/V *Eastward*. The ship, 117 feet long, with a twenty-eight-foot beam, was Duke University's research vessel. She and her crew operated out of the university's marine lab on Pivers Island and were available to various research groups. Gene Huntsman, fearless leader on this cruise, had somehow convinced the authorities that a little research should be done on the "shelf break fish community," that is, tagging, dating and studying of reef fish populations.

To me it had been presented as a free fishing trip, but signs of activities other than fun fishing loomed high, literally, and we loaded huge piles of fish traps, coils of line, nets, weights, floats, markers, and other bric-a-brac aboard the staunch *Eastward*, pushing her more firmly into the water. Gene's two henchmen, Sekavec and Manooch, better known as Glenn and Chuck, were also overseeing the loading, as the rest of the crew slaved under their watchful eyes.

A farewell meal ashore, orders read, watches established, a long, last feel of *terra firma*, and lines were cast off. The beat of the propeller quivered through the ship, and familiar landmarks began to recede. All hands mustered and we were told, "We will now have a fire drill." Seven clangs of the bell and long bonging means collision, with life jackets, rafts, and all. I was more interested in the galley, but no meals would be served until the next morning at 0730, also seven bells.

There was the slow rise and fall of the ship meeting the ocean swells. My first watch, I remembered, was 0600 to six P.M. No, it was the other way, six P.M. to 0600. The sky was gray, and the ocean, too, as we headed south, a low white beach line fading astern. A flash of pink on the western horizon, and the day was gone. Being on watch means that one is not supposed to sleep. Sleep is something that I esteem highly, along with eating. I was to learn that there was a distinct class separation on board *Eastward*: crew sits at one table, scientists at the other. There being no third table, I was classed as a scientist.

The ocean was smooth, the ship rolling lightly through the inky night. A few stars slid by the swaying topmast. Orange lightning flickered through clouds on the southern horizon. The moon, on the wane, finally lifted above the sea, a brilliant light reflected in a thousand patterns off the glossy black water. To the east, running lights of two ships moved slowly on the horizon. Our ship swung to a northeasterly heading and throbbed on, a glaring cluster of lights in an otherwise empty world.

The sun was just beginning to consider getting up when the ship's engine slowed. We lay unmoving; there was the thudding of feet on the decks and the clatter of gear. We had arrived off Cape Hatteras, the first station. Fish traps, their long lines attached to floats, splashed overboard, the traps sinking in the semi-darkness, unwinding line yard after yard. One trap pulled line and floats down with it, disappearing forever. Somewhere belowdecks a bell tinkled. Chow call, long awaited. Food being uppermost in my mind, I was nearly first in line to the shining galley. Hotcakes, bacon, custom-cooked eggs, cereals and toast, jams and coffee—the finest recommendation for a happy ship that I know.

By the time we returned on deck, the wind had risen. The chop had stirred the water to a mean-looking dirty gray, with whitecaps racing the tops of the seas. Then a sizzling, blinding rain flattened the waves into smoking, steaming liquid. At the lee rail stood our leader, with a peculiar green look. He was not alone. My locker held the expedition's supply of seasick pills. During the rest of the cruise, almost any time of day or night, I'd find a glassy-eyed, wobbly-kneed soul clutching at the locker's swinging door. He'd be pawing, grasping at the magic little pills. I considered opening a concession, but I didn't want them in the stateroom any longer than necessary.

Hours dragged on. We moved from station to station. I found myself fishing at three A.M.; I couldn't believe it. A shout from the bridge. The strange object in the water appeared to be an aircraft. The ship hove to alongside; we threw a grapnel, then worked a line through a lifting ring and winched aboard what turned out to be a drone. After banging it against hull and deck, we saw, with the aid of a flashlight, "Danger. May contain live ordnance."

The loom of Hatteras Light was abeam, the light itself still below the horizon. A quick-flashing bright light warned of Diamond Shoals off the starboard quarter. On the fathometer lumps on the bottom outlined the remains of a once-proud ship that had failed the test. The night was indescribably black: no street lights, no headlights, yard lights, security lights, just black ocean swallowing all in its gloom.

During the cruise several small birds came aboard. Flying near the ship by day, one by one they died. Some fluttered to the water, a few splashes, then merely floating feathers. A magnolia warbler landed on my shoulder; next morning it was dead. Barn swallows and a brown-backed yellow-bellied bird with small stripes also ended in forlorn heaps of feathers. The mate said they often showed up, especially after a low had passed. Blown to sea to perish on an unfathomable ocean whose waves are years, that is an inconsolable loneliness. Yet the open sea is filled with mysteries and delights, frightening in its vastness, but ultimate in its serenity.

When one feels good aboard a boat, one feels very, very good, especially after an extended period of being seasick. I stood on deck watching flying fish burst out of the indigo sea. The big-eyed silver and blue creatures would explode out of a translucent wave crest, spread their transparent pectoral "wings" and skim across the surface, only a few inches above the water. Sometimes they clipped a wave top, using it as a further springboard, and sailed on. The immensity and beauty out there is overwhelming. The clean, clear imponderable depths now seemed a metallic blue, with the surface shimmer showing a dab of luminescent violet. The ship's bow rose and fell in steady rhythm. A school of spotted porpoises passed in review, closing in on our bow wake, rising to watch us for a response, the inevitable grin on each face, then passing under the ship, racing ahead and crisscrossing.

Who ever said the sea is monotonous? Long rollers, from some faraway storm perhaps, silently came and went. A quintet of squid rose at night to lie near the surface, studying our ship, then clustered together in a ring, like football players in a strategy huddle. One broke out, looked us over and returned. A scientist made a scoop with a long-handled dipnet, but they broke, gathered again and faded into the depths. Two long-billed houndfish lay just at the edge of the light, also watching, prowling. A flying fish came too close alongside, watching like a kid seeing the circus come to town, and the net scooped it aboard. Scientists are dangerous critters.

Far below, strange blue-and-yellow forms passed, like ghosts. The cry "Dolphin!" brought spinning rods and feathers. The bull-headed "Living Color" sport of the fish world hit and ran; the light mono line sang out, and rods arched dangerously. There is no better sports fish, pound for pound, than the dolphin. Care not that the ancient Greeks and others were mixed up and didn't know the difference between a fish and a mammal. Dolphin are fast, rainbow-hued, cold-blooded fish. Porpoises are the brainy, air-breathing, warm-blooded mammals trained to jump through hoops. Dolphin, roamers of the open ocean, are speedy and tough. On reasonable tackle, they will put on a spectacular aerial display. No one has really gone deep-sea sportsfishing until he tries the dolphin on spinning tackle with ten- to fifteen-pound line, or on a flyrod. We brought perhaps a half-dozen aboard before they decided that we were inhospitable.

Our *Eastward* cruise was really scientific, with fish traps, deep-water seines and bottom fishing rigs. The latter are usually bicycle rigs, the rear wheel mechanism of an ordinary bike being inserted in a large spool, giving it both free wheeling and brakes. The pedals are replaced by handles, and, on a short spring arm and a pulley is the line, one-hundred-pound test or better, a hundred fathoms of it and two or more pounds of weights. By releasing the brake, often resulting in a few backlashes the first time or so, one drops the baited hooks to perhaps fifty fathoms. Wait for a bite, then pedal the bike like mad. One of the beauties of this kind of fishing is that one doesn't know what kind of monster will appear: sea bass, amberjack, grouper, porgy, and snapper are but a few. When the fish breaks water the fun begins.

Chuck or Glenn would be waiting to grab the flapping fish in his arms. Imagine a grown man trying to juggle a leaping porgy while running down a rocking, rolling deck. Hugging the fish to his chest, he races to the weighing station, lays it, flipping, on a board, checks its size, yelling something like, "Red porgy, so many centimeters, two pounds four ounces," and jabs a yellow tag in its back, all in one quick motion. Reading out "Tag Number So-and-so!" en route, he rushes to the rail as the log keeper duly notes all this and carefully drops the fish, bow down, back into the ocean. Somewhere along the way he has pulled a single scale of the fish with tweezers and deposited the memento in a bag.

If the racing scientist has done everything quickly enough, carefully enough, the fish will recover after an instant, flip its tail high and dive back to the depths. A very few don't make it, and the long-handled dipnet recovers them. Some fish, like groupers, almost explode from the tremendous pressure changes and seldom recover. A reward is paid to the finder of any of these tagged fish. Those that are recovered and reported help determine numbers of fish, where they live, if and where they migrate, ages and sizes, rates of growth, and the like. The future value of this information is inestimable: how much pressure from fishing can the resource stand, with our burgeoning populations and decreasing food surpluses? Can this really be a source of food for the future? Woods Hole Oceanographic Institution, in its cooperative game fish tagging program, found in blue-fin tuna tagging that great inroads were being made into the supply. A tag return of twenty-five percent indicated that not many got away. It also showed the lack of medium-sized fish, probably due to excessively heavy fishing pressures. In short, we can't count on tuna for the future. Maybe we can expect something from snappers and sea bass, though present evidence gives a dim outlook.

I don't know what all the scientists found out, but I observed that: fish traps get lost and don't catch much; conger eels have a preference for menhaden; sharks tear great holes in nets; fish don't get caught in them anywhere like I'd thought they would; nets get torn to pieces very quickly; otter trawls on rocky bottoms make about one trip, then are better forgotten; there are lots of snappers, porgies, and sea bass; English hooks bend and don't break; Norwegian hooks break and don't bend (or it may be the other way around), and Herter's hooks do both.

And scientists aren't very sporting about fish pools, the way fishermen are on headboats; I felt this strongly after I'd caught the biggest fish, an eighteen-pound strawberry grouper. I hooked bigger ones, of course, but the hooks kept straightening. I observed further that few people get seasick if they are catching fish. The *Eastward* cook, Howard, used to cook on pogy (menhaden) boats; those pogy fishermen must have eaten mighty fine. The topography of the Atlantic hasn't changed much since Eric the Red and his crew tried to keep their feet under them. Nature still rules; man adapts.

BELLY FLOWERS

By lying on one's belly and looking closely, it is possible to become aware of the little beauties that many people never see. It's only by getting close that one can appreciate the ants, the bees, the minute flowers, and the wildlife.

There is a period starting the latter part of May and running through June when fishing fever becomes a major epidemic. Fortunately, the best fishing occurs during those same weeks. The symptoms are obvious: neglect of wives, businesses, homes, lawns—everything. Some are immune— I've seen otherwise sane and normal people go on with their business just as if the fish weren't biting. And I've seen grown men walk right by a fisherman laden with his catch and not seem to notice. It has to be pretense, though, or else they are too numb from that more dread disease called work-

itis. I once knew a pier operator who had caught workitis. While giving me a rundown of fishing successes from his pier, he told me, bald-faced, that he hadn't fished in three years. His is an advanced case for which there is probably neither hope nor help.

One thing about fishing fever is hard to understand: the total and complete loss of judgment. For example, the odds against success may be a thousand to one. Yet businessmen who would squeeze a penny to the bleeding point and be utterly merciless in dealings to make a profit will casually blow thousands of dollars for a sure loss at fishing.

The best, most specific instance is the marlin fisherman, a glutton for punishment if ever there was one. In the typical tournament, like the one held every June off the Carteret Coast, about five to seven hundred men rise from their beds, bleary-eyed and possibly hung over, to dash to the boats long before the first cockcrow. Their purpose is to spend the day broiling and blistering under a near-tropic sun, bouncing and slamming around on a heaving ocean probably doing likewise, spending their thousands in a fleet of plastic and chrome worth millions, just to try to catch a fish that is considered by most of them inedible. If the fisherman does succeed, with the chances something in the neighborhood of one in a thousand, it will cost him several hundreds more by the time the fish has been mounted and the photographers paid off.

There is but one consoling feature about marlin fishing here. That is, how low the mighty will stoop. They will, after all this unbelievable effort, be rewarded with a roast mullet. True, it's a gourmet's treat that few of the common herd shall be exposed to, but is it worth the price? If put to a vote, I daresay, and this indicates the extent to which they have succumbed, there would be a unanimous vote of ayes. Yes, willingly they go out to catch the marlin and come back to eat the bait.

But marlin fishermen are not the only fevered ones. Go to a fishing pier and watch the seekers after king mackerel. An odd bunch. There may be a school of sea mullet or blues, of spots or croakers, swirling around, thick as popcorn in a flusher. But will any abandon the pier head to engage these other, even more delectable, species in combat? Not a chance! They will grip rods more tightly and stare fixedly to seaward, their bright-colored floats bobbing monotonously on the swells.

Yet most fishermen are specialists. Some pick only the channel bass and disdain the blue; others desire only trout and curse at flounder. The cobia fisherman will spend long hours hoping to lure this great fighter with treacherous bait. And there are the bait fishermen, those who will buy a bag of shrimp, those indescribably delicious crustaceans, and feed four-dollar-a-pound shrimp to tweny-five-cents-a-pound fish.

Insanity is accepted as normal for sportsfishermen. The Harpies of the sea pluck them and send them on, broke and burned, exhausted, with aching backs and red eyes. And they insist they've had a good time. Fortunately for mankind, many, especially women, are not so susceptible, and manage to keep the world going—somewhere—as the rest of the species suffers through this seasonal malady. Most victims do recover, though, if only for a little while. But once they've had this virus, they find it recurring, twice a year or more, despite valiant efforts to fend it off. There are those who never recover, those who are lost to their fellow man forever. The strange thing is that they act so happy about it.

～～～～～～～～～～～～

Though help was scarce, *Sylvia II* attracted considerable attention around the community. Wallace Guthrie, dangling bare feet over the edge of the dock, reminisced, "I 'member goin' over to Bogue Banks to help select the timber for the stem. Looked all over the woods 'fore we found one that'd suit William Riley. I was just a kid then." William Riley Willis was the owner.

"You sure this is the same boat?" I asked.

"Oh yeah. Look at the fall post. It's got a Buick hub cap." I'd noticed that the fall post (Samson post) had a cap, but hadn't paid it any attention. Sure enough, under many layers of chipped and battered paint was an ancient brass hub cap, the type that screwed on with a wrench. Showing through faintly were the bold letters BUICK.

On another occasion Jack Lewis volunteered, "Spent many a time 'board her. Five of us. Can you imagine five men sleeping in her cabin of a hot summer night a week or so at a time? We sure stunk! At night, if we could, we'd pull into a little creek somewheres and sleep on shore. That was if the weather was good. We'd do our cookin' ashore, too, if we could. But most of the time we'd be layin' to the nets. She was a top boat!" A Harkers Islander remembered when Theodore had just bought *Sylvia II*. "We'd be fishin' in Core Sound, and we could tell it was Theodore by his cigar—downwind, we could smell it a mile away. Oh, there's been many a ton of mackerel and blues aboard her! Reckon it'd fill a warehouse!"

∽∽∽∽∽∽∽∽∽∽∽∽∽

To learn about *Sylvia II* is to learn about Promise Land. Promise Land is a neighborhood of traditional fishermen on the Morehead City waterfront. Many of the early inhabitants of Morehead City had once lived on Shackleford Banks, the island lying between Beaufort Inlet and Cape Lookout. A succession of severe storms and hurricanes in the 1890s had left the small barrier island virtually uninhabitable, so the residents snaked their homes onto boats and barges and floated them to the mainland. As they passed Shepard's Point, now east Morehead City, someone hailed them for their destination. The reply echoed across placid Bogue Sound, "We're the Children of Israel, headin' for the Promise Land!" The section of the mainland shore where they settled is still known by that name.

These seafaring men, whalers and fishermen, had always built their own boats, many of which are afloat to this day. Their descendants can be found on any ocean. They are true watermen. Such a man was William Riley Willis, who, in the early 1930s, had *Sylvia II* built behind his house at the foot of 11th Street in Promise Land. He was known as "Just Right" Willis and "Double Dip" Willis, because he was such a stickler for perfection that he insisted the galvanized fastenings for the boat be double-dipped in zinc.

The boat, thirty-six feet long, nine feet in beam, and drawing twenty-seven inches, was designed as a Core Sound sink netter, often referred to as a quarter boat, that is, four feet of length for every foot of beam. She is of dead rise construction, has a sharp, straight stem and little flare. With a sharp entry until about one-third of the way aft, she flattens to a hard chine, ending in an elliptical or round, overhanging stern with a forty to forty-five degree rake. The characteristic stern is also called barrel stave, for its vertical planking.

Sylvia II is a descendant of the Carolina sharpie, a proven, easy-riding hull that knifes with a fair lift into the close, steep seas typical of North Carolina's sounds and cape shoals. Her rounded stern, in action similar to double-enders such as lifeboats, parts a following sea, making it easier to enter the shoal inlets of this coast. Narrowness makes her fast and economical and aids in keeping her dry, yet she will carry a good load under adverse conditions. Low freeboard (cightccn inchcs aft) and the overhang make her easy to work from, and the stern deck is an ideal working platform.

<hr />

It had been nearly four months since the sinking, and all systems—well, most systems—seemed go. A trip was premature, but we had to make a try. The excuse was to do some propeller work—I'd neglected to replace a nut after working on the shaft and reasoned that lying in the muddy filth beneath the boat wasn't the way to do it. I'd figured that the prop was probably frozen to the shaft, so as long as I didn't use reverse gear, I could replace the nut in clean water. To all appearances it was a sound theory, and the marina crowd wanted a party, though admittedly not a work party. There was no muffler, and the straight dry exhaust pointed heavenward. The engine, after some cranking and coaxing, emitted a black cloud of smoke. Witnesses said it looked like Vesuvius erupting (this was before St. Helens' performance). Flames and sparks spewed into the air, hot fragments of rust and scale and carbon clattered across decks and cabin top and sizzled into the water. It was as effective as a machine gun burst, sending all hands scattering for cover.

But the old Crown had made the effort. Panting, coughing, snorting, and wheezing, it finally caught on and settled down to a steady rumble, smoothing out as the engine warmed. Oil pressure was steady at forty pounds, the generator was charging, and the new temperature gauge began to rise. We tied her loose and engaged the clutch. *Sylvia II* seemed to pause as if trying to remember. There was a quiver, then a surge as she leapt forward, cleared a piling, and headed towards the sound. We anchored near Cricket Island, where we got a fire going and set good seafoods to cooking. The tide was still low, puffy clouds drifted by, and the water was warm—it was a fine party.

Long after dark we fired up the engine, hoisted anchor and idled back into the blackness of the creek. Halfway back I remembered the announced purpose of the cruise: to replace the nut after the tide got up. We glided slowly up to the dock, tied her down and congratulated ourselves. A few days later the report filtered back, "What a party you must've had! You woke up half the creek!" I'd thought we were quite sedate, though when one has only a row of pilings for a reverse gear, it might raise the question of who, if anyone, is at the helm. Well, I thought, I'd have to give Theodore that other hundred dollars. Next day Mary and I added it up: so far, after months of hard work, we had a genuine running thirty-six-foot antique boat for less than twelve hundred dollars. We knew that there was still a long way to go.

〰〰〰〰〰〰〰〰〰〰〰〰

In the back yard by the pitcher pump at the wellhead, a soft lavender and green blanket of woods violets has spread, sheltered from the sun by a live oak whose branches extend more than a hundred feet. This canopy is met by a large hickory and a black gum. Here is the squirrels' playground, and here a pair of screech owls is raising this year's hatch of two, fully feathered now and almost ready to go on their own. Violets and partridgeberries, May apples bursting like green fountains to shade the waxy white blossoms—this is belly flower country, where, by pausing even briefly and looking closely at the sprawl of color, we find the beauty almost beyond comprehension. A mockingbird is drinking from the pool formed where the pitcher pump, rusty and moss-covered, drips into a trash can lid recessed into the ground. This is the community waterhole for ducks and birds and stray dogs; hunting grounds, too, for passing hawks and falcons.

Whenever I see one of these birds of prey, I think of Falca. We found her lying in the middle of a busy highway out in Montana; she'd just been hit by a car and was such a bloody mess I thought she was dead. As we stopped, another motorist honked angrily and whipped by. Scooping her up quickly, I saw an eye open, look at me, then close. "No chance to survive. Kindest thing to do is put her out of her misery. But I can't stop now." We drove on, Mary identifying her as *Falco sparverius*, member of the falcon family known as sparrow hawk.

That evening we examined her: probably skull fracture, bleeding from bill and nostrils, one eye crushed, blood and fluid dripping, feathers turned inside out, possible wing damage, leg broken—could she survive the night? Again, we hesitated to end her suffering. Her bill was open, her tongue dry. She opened her good eye and looked at us. Three drops of water poured from a teaspoon onto her tongue. She swallowed, and I gave her a few more drops. The dull eye grew luminous. We put her in a box and covered it. Next morning she was lying on her side, watching us. I hurried to the drugstore for a medicine dropper. A few more drops of water, and the eye brightened still more. An hour or so later she opened her bill when I approached with the medicine dropper. She managed to swallow a tiny bit of raw elk liver dropped onto her mouth. By evening she accepted more liver.

Falca survived another night, and Mary reported her standing unsteadily on one foot, but not for long. The left side of her head was twice normal size, the bad eye oozing fluid, and she was gasping. Still, she took food. There was another trip to the drugstore, where the pharmacist recommended parakeet antibiotics. Another day, and again she could stand briefly on one foot. She accepted food with some relish and was able to pull her wings together. Next we gave her a box with chicken wire front and a low perch, and soon she was smacking her bill with apparent delight whenever we came near with food. She could sit, but not stand, on her perch. Her broken leg was still purple and swollen, but her head was no longer swollen. She began to accept handling without fuss and made her first flight, with a crash landing on Old Baldy, the refrigerator. Gradually, she recovered, getting as friendly as any fierce-eyed predator can get. Her favorite perch during the day became my shoulder, and she spent hours sitting there, occasionally tweaking a hair or an ear, watching me at work.

Mice, her favorite food, were hard to get. She developed a taste for them after Prof. Royal Brunson gave her a boxful of white mice that he had raised for his research at the University of Montana. At first, we cut the frozen mouse in two, because of her injuries, but soon she was able to open them and eat the whole messy critters. I can't say much for her taste. Mice were dessert. Liver, kidney, any rich meat, was basic, and small dead birds or road kills. She disdained grasshoppers. It always gave me a sense of achievement to walk onto the screened porch she owned, with a piece of meat in my hand, to whistle to her and see her sweep swiftly towards me on widespread wings. She'd drop gently onto my arm, clutching with needle-tipped talons and never breaking the skin. Then she'd slice the meat neatly from between my fingers without once touching me. After a while we tried teaching her to catch her own mice, but they were hard to come by. I could never perfect the swoop and dive myself, and even with the help of Fang, the family dog, the mouse always seemed to come up the winner. Falca enjoyed the show, though.

One day she had a visitor. Sitting on my shoulder, she began to mutter and flew out to the porch. A male falcon (we falconers call them tercels) came whistling in from on high and landed in the fig tree. They had a little chat. Mary interpreted it as a visit from an old boyfriend saying, "Falca, you're hard to find. I had a dickens of a time following that blue canoe all the way from Montana. And going through Chicago after dark, well!" My view was that he was simply a southern gentleman paying his respects to the new gal from the West.

Then came that wild and windy late spring day. Falca was restless. Suspecting her boyfriend was somewhere near, I took her out, as was the custom, for a bit of fresh air. There was a faint "Kreee," barely audible above the wind through the trees. Falca rose in spiraling flight, up and up, far beyond her normal flight pattern. The wind may have confused her. Then we saw another bird circling. They faded into the hazy sky, and Falca was gone. I doubt that she could have survived long, with only one eye and accustomed now to easy living. Yet, every once in a while, when we hear the sound of a soft "Kreee," we wonder if she has come back just for a visit.

It does seem that man should have the right to have wildlife in his life. When the Lord built the pocosins, the marshes, swamps, and creeks, there was a reason, just as much a reason as to create man and give him a mind. But today wildlife is disappearing from this country at a rate of one species a year. Now it took the Creator quite a few eons to design and improve the system, with its ivory-billed woodpeckers, manatees, bald eagles, fringed gentians, and pupfish. Seems mighty narrow-minded for man to usurp all the living room and deny others the right to life.

〰〰〰〰〰〰〰〰〰

I have just come back from my dawn survey of the shore and an investigation of what was panicking the ducks. The cause of all the commotion was four juvenile river otters cavorting in the creek, chirping at one another, rising out of the water to their shoulders to look me over. The sight of them brings it all back vividly.

Mary and I had returned late one night, dead tired from a turkey hunt, to find a welcoming committee sitting on the back step: my brother Bill, our young neighbor Kim Wilson, and our little squirrel dog Fang. It seemed strange that they should wait up for us until almost midnight just to see that we got home all right, for our outings were commonplace.

I was too tired to give it a second thought, but the moment we stepped into the kitchen I caught a distinct scent of musk. The closer I came to the bathroom, the stronger the odor. I opened the bathroom door and followed my nose to the tub. There were splashes. I pulled back the shower curtain and saw what looked like a scrawny black rat staring back at me. Mary and Kim and Bill crowded close behind. No, it wasn't a rat. A beaver? Too black, and it had a long, pointed tail with fur. An otter!

Then the story poured out: Kim had been swimming in the creek that morning, floating on her back in the warm waters, thinking young girl thoughts, when she felt something crawling up on her flippers. (Kim is a normal shore species, not a mermaid, and her flippers were the rubber type.) It was a small animal, apparently in imminent danger of drowning, and was struggling to find safety. Assisting the little critter ashore, Kim called my brother, who was mending a net nearby. Bill scooped the animal into a bucket and deposited it in our bathtub—not hers, not his. Ours was closest, and unguarded. They began the long wait for our return.

It was unnerving to have those beady black eyes glaring, frightened, angry, defensive. He was a rack of bones, too. There was no privacy in our bathroom any more. Fact is, for a while it was the neighborhood social center. Mary found a medicine dropper, filled it with warm milk, and offered it to the black waif. He didn't appreciate her efforts and hissed a little. It was then that I took charge, pulling on a pair of welder's gloves, diverting the little fellow with a towel in order to grab him. He grabbed me with as wicked set of incisors as I'd encountered in a long time. But a few squirts of milk, shot into his mouth while he was looking for a place to bite me, seemed to lessen his rage slightly. And then I realized, from the ribs so prominent under the loose hide, the pinched face of bone and skin, how long-starved he was.

Next morning we trotted off to the drugstore to get baby bottles and set about feeding him. Immediately he bit off the nipple and wasn't really much interested in the milk. Meanwhile, I was studying reference books for diet hints. An offering of fish cleanings went a bit better, but it was necessary to force-feed him. To force-feed a fast, razor-toothed wild animal is akin to jabbing at a rotating buzz saw.

The bathtub ultimately being needed for other purposes, we gave the otter—now called Otto by unanimous vote—new quarters in the same small screened porch that had housed Falca. Within a few days he began to calm down. He'd weighed in originally at a shy three pounds. He showed a marked preference for live minnows, which were in short supply. We offered him boiled egg, liver, and fish roe as emergency rations.

Within a week he grew noticeably relaxed and seemed to like having his ears scratched. As long as one moved very slowly he gave only friendly bites, mostly about the ankles. Preferring to stay in the mainstream of life, he was shortly given the run of the house; only, however, after he had proved to housebreak himself. (He used a large bucket of water for his toilet, a second bucket for splashing—a fastidious little animal.)

Eeling along like an inch-worm to the sofa where we did most of our writing and reading, he'd offer his ears for scratching, then climb up a leg to curl up alongside for only a few seconds until he was ready to explore or play. The sofa was also the domain of our small, multiancestored dog, who resented Otto's trespassing. Often it was necessary to break up the resulting impasse.

As time passed he developed a pot belly and had lost some of his initial fears. Still, any sudden movement or noise would send him into a panic. He'd head under a bearskin rug, emerging only long after the disturbance had passed. His appetite was growing at a remarkable rate, and just to obtain small fish became a major effort. We'd beg anything from passing fishermen, drag a minnow net, and scour local fish houses. The handful of minnows it took a half-hour to catch would make possible two meals, so long as there was no waiting time between. And our dog Fang, hitherto much too sophisticated to eat such things, decided that the fish had merit and would eagerly assist in the consumption of the supply.

Within a very short time Otto had regained his health and decided that he wanted his freedom, too. He began to chew his way through the porch screen. Bill intercepted him and nailed a piece of plywood over the hole. At the end of the day he had all but enclosed the porch. We decided, not without some pangs of regret—by now the little fellow had become almost a member of the family—that if he wanted his freedom, he could have it. After all, he was a wild animal, and if he didn't appreciate our hospitality, that was his right. I scratched his ears and explained to him that things weren't all roses and free fish out there, that there were dogs and boats and people. Then I opened the porch door, and he bounded down the steps, looked about, and loped happily across the yard. Our semi-wild ducks flew frantically in every direction.

By this time he and Fang and Bill's beagle, Pat, had become pretty good friends, wrestling and playing incessantly. Pat romped out to join him in a free-for-all. To our surprise, after a few minutes of play, a quick swim in a rain tub, and an exploration beneath the house, Otto demanded to be let back in. He headed directly for the dog's bowl. From that time on, he had complete freedom on request.

In the upbringing of this otter pup, I found it necessary to read widely on all sorts of wildlife lore. I learned that, while much of an otter's life is guided solely by instinct, one thing Ma Nature leaves up to the otter mother is teaching the pups how to fish. This was a surprise to me. I'd always presumed that these things were as natural as breathing. The book said further that they even have to be taught to swim.

Otto already knew how to swim, but it became clear that if he were to be independent, and relieve me of some of my obligations, he would have to be taught how to fish. The thought stirred pleasant reveries. I could see it vividly: as I prepared the fry pan, I'd whistle to Otto and say, "Go fetch us a fish. I prefer trout, but a blue will do." Otto would lope to the creek, and, in a matter of minutes, we could be enjoying a fresh-fried trout for breakfast. This fellow's going to be handy, I thought, and earn his way. The best the dog can do is to tree a squirrel or chase a rabbit, but here is a real hunter, easily trained.

Training was the weak point. The first step was to enter the water and catch a fish to show how it's done. At least, I figured, his mama

66

would have demonstrated. I had learned through early experience that it is difficult to catch a fish by hand, much less by teeth, as his mother would have done. Otto and I waded into the creek. This was great! He'd roll and loop, his catfish-like face all a-grin, white whiskers twitching, black eyes glittering. I'd approach what I deemed a good minnow hideout, shake the grasses and weeds, and hand him a minnow that I'd previously secreted in my pocket. He would accept and dash off here and there in glee, to pick up a bright piece of shell or a shiny pop top. He seemed to think that food comes from stores, as do some humans unable to connect soil, water, cows, and grass with milk, vegetables, beef, and even fish. To Otto, milk still came from the refrigerator and fish from the freezer.

Now that he was requiring three pounds or more a day, it was important that he quit diving for chromed scrap and ignoring all the fish swimming by. I was finding it very difficult to set an example, and passing boatmen surely thought it strange to see a mighty thrashing about, then a human posterior poking out of the shallows, and two moustached creatures rising from the depths. I recalled that we once had a duck that had to be taught to swim.

Bill's suggestion made the lessons successful. We stretched a minnow net into the channel, securing one end ashore. I whistled for Otto, and together we entered the creek. This time Bill pulled the end of the net ashore, shortening the bunt until Otto and I were surrounded by a school of flashing, panic-stricken shiners and some larger pinfish. Otto became excited, fascinated by all the shiny toys flitting about. He began to pursue, with almost immediate success. To swim with an otter is to observe the phenomenal speed and grace of a fully streamlined body. Never again did I worry about his self-sustaining capabilities.

Besides, he had already become the pet of the neighborhood. Sportsfishermen passing by would fling a fish or two ashore whenever they saw him playing. Kids from all around were riding their bikes down our dusty lane, through a tunnel of trees, to knock on the door: "Please, can I play with Otto?" Of course, proud Kim, who spent every spare moment with him, was encouraging them to come see *her* pet otter.

Our hearts were touched many times to see two or three ten- to twelve-year-olds playing in the water with this black bullet gliding among their feet, standing on his hind legs, begging them to join him, while two rather sedate dogs sat on shore watching with disapproval. Still, Otto was a wild animal, and there was a distinct possibility that he would revert to wild ways, feel a need to defend himself, and respond with razor teeth. We watched the kids closely.

The availability of fish ceased to be of concern after Otto decided that dry dog food couldn't be all bad if Fang ate it. For her part, Fang concluded that frozen mullet must have something in its favor if Otto liked it. The otter was direct, but Fang was a shrewd, calculating female. It was doubtful that she could have bested the otter in a fight, and she must have known it. But she had observed that if a strange dog came into the yard and she chased after it, Otto would drop anything and dive for sanctuary under the house. Shortly we realized that there weren't nearly as many dogs about as Fang chased off. She'd sit watching as I handed Otto a mullet, frozen hard as a rock, but he could bite through it as if it were an overripe banana, devouring it in moments as he sat erect, holding it between his forepaws. Fang always watched these proceedings squinty-eyed, as if half asleep. If I disappeared, she'd leap off the porch, barking wildly at what we came to call "The Phantom of Soggy Bottoms," her imaginary intruder. And Otto never learned: each time he'd drop the fish and go for cover. Fang would trot back smugly, pick up the fish, and be finishing it off, licking the last scale from her whiskers, by the time Otto poked a wary head out from under the porch.

As he grew older, Otto grew bolder and became wise in the ways of humans, who provided food and fun and slept late. Until we, too, became wiser, we found ourselves being awakened long before sunup, while the mists were still shrouding the horizons. There'd be the slam of the kitchen screen door, the "clumpety-clumpety" of four legs racing through the kitchen, across the living room, and into the bedroom. Rolling over, we'd find ourselves face to face with a mischievous black countenance, eyes shining, whiskers quivering, paws clutching the edge of the bed. It was a showdown, eye to eye, nose to nose, and we knew that if we didn't get out of bed at once, we'd be overrun by (now) twenty pounds of soaking-wet otter just out of the creek and ready for a grand romp. Playtime at five-thirty A.M. is not much better than a mad wife.

It's the same old story of men and critters: we want to own, to possess, to make animals, wild and domestic, dependent on us. It seems to enhance our sense of worth. We cry for our freedom and want to deny them theirs. Friendship with animals should be one of mutual respect. It cannot be bought or demanded by collar and chain, for this is slavery of wild things that are valuable if we have any regard for freedom ourselves.

Otters are kin to skunks. We'd never noticed any objectionable odor since the first day Otto had arrived, starved and frightened and shut up in the bathroom. No, he was scrupulously clean and well-mannered. But there was one thing that terrified him, and that was an internal combustion engine. The engine of a close-passing boat was enough to put him into a deep dive or a scramble for the marsh. An automobile would send him under the house. He recognized our car, but always stayed a safe distance away whenever we went near it.

Then one day a local doctor brought his two kids to meet Otto. They were all introduced and played together happily until it was time to go. I scooped Otto into my arms and walked with the family to their car. We talked a few minutes and the doctor started the engine with a roar. Otto clutched me in fright and at once I became aware of a strong stench, a musky odor not much less obnoxious than a skunk's best effort. The doctor drove off in a hurry, if not in a high dudgeon. An encyclopedia of wildlife describes otters as members of the *muskadia* family—and it isn't kidding.

Whenever I saw that shining black form lying in the yard, bright eyes studying me, it was hard to think of him as wild, especially when a short time before he'd banged at the door, pulled it open, and nosed his way inside. He'd peered around before making happily for the bearskin rug in front of the fireplace, rolling in it, crawling beneath to hide for a bit, watching me, then, with utmost stealth, sliding across the floor to pounce onto the sofa in mock attack as I sat writing. White whiskers twitching, he'd looked up at me earnestly before beginning to munch reflectively on the eraser end of the pencil.

But I was at work and couldn't be bothered. I tried to ignore him, then pushed him away with my left hand, which he grabbed to wrestle. I tried scratching his belly to calm him, meanwhile still attempting to concentrate. He chewed on my ring, tugged at my watch, but soon dropped my hand to flop his warm, loose-skinned body across the writing pad. Temporarily contented, he lay still for little more than a moment before beginning to explore the hair on my arm. Next he was draping himself over my neck and shoulders, nibbling gently at my ear (now this made me nervous; I knew he was tame and trusting, but still—).

Finally, he dozed off briefly, but was up again soon, eeling across my knee to the coffee table, steadying himself on his forepaws to nose into a bowl and sniff at a rose. Satisfied that there was no action there, he took a flying leap at Fang, who'd been sleeping peacefully on the floor. A great wrestling and snarling match ensued, soon cut short by Mary's booting both of them out of the house.

Mary was the disciplinarian, handling the punishment if it were needed. She'd belt him a solid one if he got into a cupboard or onto a table. For the most part, he was good-natured about it all—nothing ventured, nothing gained. His vocabulary was limited, but understandable. A small, almost bird-like chirp indicated happiness and playfulness, his usual humor. A hiss said that he was disturbed. A hissing bark said anger, and was sure to get him cuffed and quickly tossed outside.

Once he picked up a small turkey Mary had put out to cool. She spoke to him sharply and he handed it back to her. She set it on a kitchen table, but he'd followed her in and was soon on a chair en route to the turkey again. She gave him a warning "Ah! Ah!," which says the same thing in any language. He retired and she put the turkey on top of the refrigerator. He took another tack: into the living room, over the sofa onto the divider, and almost within reach of the turkey when Mary snatched him and carried him to the door. By this time he was nearing thirty pounds, and she needed both hands. An otter's hide is attached only at the tip of the nose, the bottom of the feet and the base of the tail. Mary found herself at the door with her arms full of loose skin and a revolving ball of muscle inside. Still, he was very fond of her. Whenever she'd open the refrigerator, he'd be hanging onto her leg like a child, watching and peering inside to see what the choices were.

The predominant feature of otters that makes them outstanding in their relations with man is their sense of fun. Anything goes until proved otherwise. They are optimistic, curious, with a sense of humor that never quits. This is not anthropomorphism on the part of the writer. Otto could and did play every waking moment, and he soon learned how to handle humans. Realize first that otters are exceedingly fast and strong. Remember that Otto could hold a two-pound frozen mullet two or three inches thick and bite through it in a single clip—no gnawing, no chewing, as efficient as a bolt cutter. Now, imagine that you are sitting in a rocker or on a sofa, dozing or concentrating on a book. Your shoes and socks are off. Here comes this sleek, furred bundle of fun, full of frozen fish and ready for action. He sees his chance and, quick as a flash, dives for the bare foot. He chomps down on that naked, defenseless big toe with those pearly bolt cutters and has both paws firmly around your foot. Oh! you can see the grin, the humor-filled eyes laughing at you. He knows he has you, and he knows you know it. Don't move!

This happened to me repeatedly until I quit taking off shoes and socks. Each time I couldn't help getting cold chills, but there was nothing I dared do. His expression was one of great delight, yet he never broke the skin—never an abrasion. It was a firm grip I knew I couldn't shake loose even if I'd dared try. It didn't last long, only a few moments, though it seemed forever. Then, still full of the devil, Otto would jump on my lap to wrestle, giving me a chance to slide into shoes or sit on my feet.

This instinct for bare feet was even more fun—for him—when he caught someone swimming. It was my habit to go to the creek around high tide, swim to the edge of the channel, roll over on my back, and take up serious cloud watching. While swallows skimmed the water, picking up insects, I'd halfway doze off. Sooner or later I'd suddenly become aware that I wasn't alone: Otto was stalking toes, big toes only, either foot. He'd surface maybe ten or twelve feet away and study for just a second before diving out of sight in the dark waters. He'd reappear in a great surging attack, straight for the big toe. I learned his timing and just when to snatch my foot away. He'd always eyeball the foot he was aiming for, and, if I watched closely enough, I could usually outguess him. Strangely, every time he missed he'd go into paroxysms of glee, virtually spinning in his excitement and chirping happily while circling for another try.

I recall a time when we'd had some problem with prowlers. Late one night I heard a suspicious noise. Putting on my bathrobe and picking up flashlight and pistol, I eased out into the yard. Standing in the cold, wet grass, peering into the blackness and listening, I was abruptly and forcibly seized by the big toe. Did I yell, throw the flashlight in the air? I don't remember, but for a moment I knew the devil had me good. It was Otto, of course. He danced about me in raptures, and he was surely rolling on his back and holding his sides as I stomped back into the house. Fortunately, most of the visitors he surprised were too civilized to come a-calling barefoot.

It was late summer, and we'd just returned from one of many trips I was making then as field director of the Wildlife Federation. Bill and Kim always kept an eye on the house, dogs, ducks, and otter for us, but, as when Otto first came on the scene, they didn't usually wait up for us. There they sat on the back steps again, both fighting back tears and trying to console each other. Alarmed, I asked, "What's wrong?"

"Otto's gone!"

"What happened?"

"Dunno. He hasn't been home for three days. Hasn't touched his food. Something awful's happened!"

We were stricken, and it was just dawning on us how much we had become attached to the lovable little fellow. "We've looked everywhere!" sobbed Kim. Standing there, trying to figure what could be done, I saw something moving from beneath the porch, a mud-spattered black face looking up, rather sadly, I thought, but with a decided what's-all-the-fuss expression. I pointed, and sad tears turned to joy. Later we deduced that Otto must have decided to go courting and been bitten by a competitor. He had applied his own mud packs over a deep slash nearly two inches long from forehead to nose. He may have been too young to court, but his instincts told him to retreat under the darkest corner of the house and plaster cool, wet healing mud on his wounds. I like to think that when he heard my voice he came out to let us know he wasn't all the way gone. A few bites of food, a washdown in his favorite swimming tub, and he disappeared for two days more, coming out only once for food and drink and to replace his mud pack. The long gash healed, leaving a noticeable scar. He stayed pretty close for several days, but as time went on we'd get reports of him from up and down the sound, though he was seldom gone for more than a day.

Cold weather was to prove no bother to Otto. His dense fur was adequate for anything. Snow, uncommon on our coast, was a source of great fun, for sliding, tunneling, or plowing. Even the occasional sheet of skim ice on the creek was made just for his pleasure. He would take great running slides, gamboling along, chasing the ducks without showing any interest in anything but making them fly, while he slid on and on.

All things must end, and Otto's career ended in a trap set by a biologist vexed at having raids made on the University of North Carolina's marine lab fish tank. His body was mounted for display in the State Museum of Natural History, and young Kim led a school bus load of youngsters to the museum to pay their respects.

Over the years we've had our share of pets—dogs that hunted, and didn't, and no-account ones; cats, horses, birds; the injured and orphaned. But never has there been any creature that approached Otto for infiltrating our affections. It seems even today that we were singularly honored when he chose to live with us. There is no way to describe how close he became, how much he opened our eyes to the freedom of the wild, to a sense of humor and play. It was a rare privilege to enjoy the respect of such an intelligent wild thing.

SHORT NIGHTS AND EASY LIVING

Nights are short and living is easy when everything reaches a vernal peak in June. Gardens are lush, flowers are blooming, fruit is on the trees.

The days are about as long as they can get now. Last winter the sun was setting behind a tower on the beach to the southwest. Now it bears to the north of west. My nautical almanac says that around noon on the 21st of June the sun's declination is 23° 26′ north of the equator, ending the last leg of its north'ard trip. On the 20th of March, between five and six in the afternoon, or thereabouts, it crossed the equator, and from the 21st of June it will be southbound. If one happens to be in the north country, above 66°, as at Fort Yukon, the sun doesn't set; it just skirts the horizon.

Indians call this the Moon of Short Nights. Northern Scandinavians celebrate the absence of evil spirits. Ducks and geese are busy taking advantage of the absence of night to produce a new crop of waterfowl, to feed in the mosquito- and black-fly-laden marshes of tundra and stunted forest. It is a land of unbelievable activity. The intensity of life is difficult to comprehend, with but a few short weeks to accomplish production quotas before shortening days signal the end.

I know these are universal truths, but I had to check on the sun today. Digging out the sextant, I pointed it to the south and cranked the mirrored image of the sun until it lay split on the far horizon. Carefully, I checked my watch for the one o'clock position, being forced to accept man's, rather than God's, time. The aging sextant of ivory and ebony and brass indicated the sun had reached 78° 30′ in height above the horizon. The ancient instrument that came off an old sailing vessel of the 1850s had read 53° 19′ in March, and in December 30° 50′ above the horizon.

Relieved to learn that the earth was still on course, and exhausted from this seasonal effort, I retreated to a vigorous stint at testing the hammock. Before long the mosquitoes moved in, and there was nothing to do but escape by way of a slow cruise. Shortly, Mary had the wicker basket packed with choice specimens of chicken and supporting supplies. We tied the boat loose and pointed her bow towards the sparkling waters of the sound. Soon she was swinging on her anchor, rocking slightly in the flooding tide that was near its crest. Dancing waves covered the shoals as the currents poured over all but a small, grassy island. Flights of gulls, returning from inland fields, swept by. Terns rested on the island. Skimmers wheeled over, giving their plaintive call. A lone pelican glided in on silent wings.

The breeze died with the sun. It was warm, humid, and silent but for the intermittent call of a bird and the chatter of water along the hull. A hazy dusk brought out a growing plethora of lights along the shores. Scarcely any bit of shoreline is truly dark today, as busy builders and speculators gobble the last of the isolation. The Fish and Wildlife Service reports handling thirty-five thousand permit applications a year to devour the rest. How long can it last?

76

Far down the sound the blinking lights of Waterway markers flashed, seeming to float above the haze. Our anchor light cast a pale illumination on the decks as we sat in the cockpit, watching the darkness enfold. Above, stars glittered. Passing boats, red and green running lights glowing, rocked us in their wakes. Storm clouds were building in the west. The forecast of rain seemed accurate, for lightning lashed in bursts of gold and ice blue within the approaching clouds. The wind was picking up, and the stars were no longer visible. Lifting anchor and retiring to the lee of our lonesome pine seemed advisable. The Thunder Moon was crowding in on the Moon of Short Nights.

Ashore it is the year of the plum. Some seasons the beach plums are hanging thick and heavy. Or there may be two or three years with none at all. They are the first to blossom in spring, filling the air with a delicately sweet scent. Great numbers of blossoms do not necessarily mean great volumes of fruit: last year a plenitude of blossoms turned into three edible plums. It's one of the risks of living the good life, which includes living off the land.

Mind you, everybody lives off the land. It's just that some folks have their food handled a lot more before they get to it. In our more direct way, we set a net in the bay in front of our cottage. It's a short one, maybe twenty-five yards. We checked it this morning, and will check it again this evening. This morning it yielded two or three croakers, a couple of jumping mullet, and quite a few menhaden. Locally they're called shad or pogies. They go into the crab pots, which may catch no more than a half-dozen crabs—which, when added to a menu of fresh fish, especially a trout or a blue, add up to some pretty good meals.

On the bank just above the net, a tangle of greenbriars grows around the live oaks and hollies. The tips of greenbriars are young, tender, and delicious. We just snap off the ends, often eating them on the spot. Another greenbriar, or smilax, looks like the head of a purple snake. This, too, is tender, and when boiled is much like asparagus. Add to this pokeweed—there's plenty of it wherever the earth has been disturbed—for greens. Away down South they call it "poke sallet." A gourmet can find no better eating in the finest restaurants.

Step out your own back door and you may find as much food as we've discovered behind our cottage. The clearing is one big bed of violets. A mint bed comes to life every spring, and a dead willow harbors oyster mushrooms. The front yard is filled with dock and lamb's quarters and wild onions. We've grown good crops of these ever since I decided that lawn mowing is the second greatest waste of time ever invented. There are several occupations that tie for first place. I'd planned to buy a couple of sheep to keep the grass down, but the Commissioner of Agriculture has never come up with a source of supply, and I've not found any around here. The theory is to let the sheep mow grass all summer. Then we eat mutton in the fall and wear sheepskin coats all winter.

Free living, of course, includes clams and shrimp for added variety, and right next to the boat there's dessert, a self-sustaining briar patch full of dewberries. Dewberries are blackberries that live on the ground, or blackberries are dewberries that grow on bushes. I'm no botanist, but I know that these are an unendangered species, being well protected by thorns and chiggers (redbugs). And there's a keg of wild cherry wine, or vinegar, in the back yard for the asking. First try, I failed to remove the pits, and the wine, or vinegar, is what you might call embittered. Beautiful color, though—a clear rich red.

Luckily, my wife puts her talents to converting some of the wild sweet cherries into jam, as she does with crab apples. If I can beat the squirrels to them, I'll pick up a few pecans and hickory nuts next fall; but they're hardly a dependable source of free food except for the squirrels. A slingshot applied to the little varmints would make more sense. As it is, they give the dog her best exercise. Oh yes, and there's yaupon tea. We find the leaves good at any season. The yaupon holly is close kin to the South American *maté*. It makes a green tea that is good for whatever ails you.

We'd had our initiation into living off the land when we first became self-unemployed. We learned quickly the ins and outs of being independently poor, first of all, by the simple admission that we were free-lancers, a title which always sounds good on paper. An unoccupied branch of Peltier Creek was not far from town and provided a sheltered anchorage in any weather. Thin times weren't unusual, and there weren't many welfare programs then. If there had been, pride probably wouldn't have let us accept food stamps or other public doles. The employment office considered me "overeducated" for shoveling fish.

There was nearly complete privacy in our branch of the creek, except for two small, broken-down fish boats and their equally broken-down owners, a pair of resident otters raising their young, and an alligator or two. In those times, I remember, Mary perfected baked beans. Down east of Beaufort in the village of Atlantic we'd found a diminutive cast-iron Shipmate fisherman's stove, measuring perhaps fifteen by twenty-one inches, with a nine-inch oven. We paid ten dollars for it and sold our alcohol "yacht" stove for fifteen dollars. By good fortune, a neighboring housing development had all the small scrap wood we could use, and there was an abundance of hardwoods lying about in the woods nearby. The stove kept us warm by winter and cooked, with Mary's aid, some of the best eating anyone could want. As a kid in the Dakotas, through dust bowl and depression, I'd been raised on potato soup, jack rabbit, and pheasant. Carolina was easy living.

As I recall, our income averaged less than forty dollars a month. To this day, I can't figure how we paid for the boat with no income to speak of. We'd bought *Silver Spray* for twenty-five hundred dollars, and the down payment had taken all of our reserve. We'd had to insure the boat in order to get a bank loan, the first the bank had ever made on any but a work boat. But beans and oatmeal were cheap. The rest came from land and sea. Clams, oysters, scallops, and crabs were basic, as were mullet and other fishes. Along the sound farmers were generous and would swap, or sell reasonably, fresh corn, cucumbers, tomatoes, and cantaloupe—Bogue Sound melons were, and still are, famous.

Mostly we depended on scrounge: swap clams for yams, help haul a beach seine and supplement cornbread with pompano, the highest-priced fish on the market. We even tried cattail flour and sassafras tea. In midsummer Mary would don heavy clothes and insect repellent (sulphur is cheap and very effective on chiggers) to forage a supply of wild blackberries, which she served in shortcake or made into jam. Seediest stuff I ever ate, but the best-tasting. She baked flounder in the oven, and biscuits. Sourdough hotcakes came right off the stovetop. Coquina clam broth was an elixir too good for the gods, and there was nothing you could do wrong to a hard crab.

Come fall there'd be sweet potatoes fried and oysters baked, or the other way around. With dove season, we could make up for the few scrawny chickens we'd been able to afford. One waterfowl season—we had a Labrador retriever then, named Pepper—Mary picked off a duck with the .22 pistol to end a recurring meat shortage. The dog barked joyfully as if to say, "You done good!" but she had to pull in the dinghy, put him in it, and row him to where he could lean over the side and retrieve the duck easily. He was no good—hated water and learned to scrounge on his own. He had a friend who kept him supplied with bones and scraps. We learned later that he'd sometimes brazen his way into the grocery store, where the manager was always very prompt in giving him scraps to keep him from frightening the customers. I'd always suspected there was a touch of the con in him.

Showers were by buckets of water we tossed over each other while standing on the stern deck. In winter it was more difficult. Yet these were the best of years, and by rare luck, we knew it then, too, for it gave us time for woods walking, watching the flowers grow and the birds migrate, learning about fish and shellfish, how to mend a net, build a crab pot, and identify a plant. Perhaps the most rewarding of all was the opportunity to get acquainted with the down-to-earth working folks who grow the corn, build the houses, dig the ditches, and catch the fish, to find out what was worth while and what wasn't. It gave us a chance to learn about Down East in North Carolina.

We found Down East to be the section of North Carolina Down

East of Beaufort, where folks still live in harmony with the sea. To be precise, a Downeaster is best defined as one who prefers salt fish (notably spots) for breakfast. But mostly it is a state of mind, where the people like wooden boats and build them in back yards beneath big live oak trees. It is where women are sensible enough to wear calico sunbonnets while out hoeing collards in a garden fenced with fishnet. It is where men still gather in the lee of an old shed, wearing rubber boots, to tell yarns as long as your arm and drink what they still call sodas. Down East is where you can see a black hunting dog dozing amid old decoys stacked carelessly beside a nethouse.

Down East Carolina is where rust-streaked skiffs rock easily, tethered to stakes in the shallows, while a soft wind ripples the sounds into hills and valleys of blues and greens and beyond is the yellow glare of sand and salt haze and sun. It is where gulls noisily follow trawlers and long haulers, their decks piled high with jumbles of nets. It's where the sharp scents of salt and marsh linger in the light, damp air. It is great stacks of crab pots and fish boxes lining the docks and kids pedaling their bicycles on sandy roads. It's men going barefoot all summer, tough-footed on shelly shores and grassy lawns, men who don't seem to mind getting up while the stars are bright to set a net or pick up a line of crab pots whose floats dot off across the sound to where horizon blends with rising sun.

Down East? Why, that's where the folks still walk along the roads at night to visit with friends sitting on porches, and gather every Sunday in church to sing together and pray together. Downeasters are the hard-working people who make up the backbone of the land, independent, strong, and proud, the salt of the earth. So whenever you visit the region located somewhere east of Beaufort, where you can watch the sun rise boldly from the sea, feel sand between your toes, and inhale the pungence of fish and brine, of marsh and pine, you may, by watching closely, find a land of dreams that is no fantasy land, but Down East.

Such is the country that can teach easy living. When we moved ashore we continued and improved our system, sometimes in ways we hadn't anticipated. One miserable day I was sitting in front of the open fire, feet propped up. The dogs were asleep on the bearskin rug, and all of us were basking in warmth and cheer. A few bars of "Born Free" were running through my mind when my brother strutted in and handed me a truffle hound, all decked out in ribbon trim. For a long time I'd dreamed of having an English setter like the one we had many years before, or maybe another Labrador to replace old Pepper. But when Bill announced that it was sure enough a truffle hound, both dogs leaped to their feet, laid back their ears, and growled. One a squirrel dog, the other a rabbit dog, they would have no truck with truffle types. In response, the truffle hound laid back its ears, narrowed beady eyes, curled its tail, and said, "Oink!"

"Her name," said Bill, "is Matilda, and she likes to sleep in your lap." Immediately after that bit of enlightenment, he departed for a Caribbean cruise, leaving us with three hounds, one with cloven hooves. I promptly took to studying books on truffles and truffle hounds. From what I could determine, truffles are found mainly in France and are eaten largely by Frenchmen, except for small amounts of the essence, which they export at outlandish prices to status-seeking Americans. The owners of truffle hounds lead the beasts around on leashes to sniff out the truffles that skulk underground. I have found out since that, despite assertions that truffles have not been discovered in North America, they do exist in the Beartooth Mountains of Wyoming. I have verification on the subject from a distinguished botanist and an equally qualified zoologist, and I tested them on three backpackers from Spokane, who were still in good health the next morning.

While Matilda never got around to detecting a truffle, she did prove to be of some worth. Five years earlier my wife had laid out a garden plot and had been nagging me every spring to dig it up and plant it. Matilda Hamhock (her full name) practiced her truffle hunting there. No longer did I have to worry about excuses like upsetting the ecological balance, or borrowing my neighbor's rototiller, or sharpening the spading fork. As steadily as a bulldozer, Matilda plowed and replowed the site, and added a bit of fertilizer at random.

Mary could have her garden after all, if she really wanted it. As for myself, I prefer natural foods, like apples and nuts and grapes, that hang conveniently from trees and vines, as well as fish and ducks, with an occasional dash of venison and, of course, beans—with hamhocks. I felt that I could easily do without truffles, and was confident that a pig parlor might well assure us of continued privacy and tranquil living, so long as the wind didn't shift.

Soon we concluded that Matilda should be trained to hunt something besides truffles, at which she'd shown no talent. Gene Huntsman had informed us that pigs can be trained to point quail, or so he'd read somewhere. This was confirmed—that he'd read it somewhere. I began looking for a trainer, the only one I knew nearby being Calico Jack McCann over on Harkers Island. I'd watched him working quite successfully with retrievers. As a former swimming coach he should be good at whipping trainees into shape, but, on the other hand, he might get no results at all, Matilda already having demonstrated that she was passable at pointing, without showing any inclination whatever to retrieve. So much for that theory.

Swine (this seems a harsh name for the gentle Matilda, who only the morning before had bitten my wife) do have certain areas in which they can be educated. My veterinarian friend George Brandt told me of a farmer who taught his pigs to march in formation to music. He marched them right into the abattoir. The idea began to have some appeal, the more I thought about it. Matilda had failed at truffling and showed no promise at all as a retriever. Still, she was extremely efficient as a combination garbage disposal, fertilizer, composter, rototiller, and entertainer of all visitors.

Matilda had been warned repeatedly that she was eating herself to an early end. But she ignored the warnings, blinking the long lashes that hid her little eyes, grunting her usual song of "How about some more chow, bub?" With the onset of hot weather our nostrils were being assaulted, so we called on our organic farmer friend Brad, who'd been raised on a Carolina tobacco farm and claimed to know about hog killings. Now hog killings and obstetrics have one thing in common, and that's hot water. The old story of the prospective father boiling pot after pot of water while wife delivers I've always discounted as a means of keeping the male out of the way. But come hog killing time, such is not the case. It takes tubs and barrels of the stuff, heated over a wood fire. And there's that other part I hadn't thought out in advance: a hog weighs a lot more than it appears to. Even before all the rituals of the ceremonial Arabian sword properly defiled, the lifting, the dipping, the scraping and groaning, I'd found my partner getting weak—green, actually. I realized then that, while he was an organic farmer, Brad didn't go to bed with the chickens. His night owl habits had kept him up until nearly sunrise, and he wasn't much help.

The next morning we placed the cooled carcass, carefully wrapped, in the front seat and took it to the block of our favorite butcher, El Nelson. El looked over the pink-skinned form in its shroud and patted it tenderly on the flank. He took off his cap for a moment and, cleaver in the other hand, sighed, "Poor Matilda!" After finishing the dissection, El hung up white cap and apron, put the razor-edged knives back in the rack, laid aside the cleaver, and put on a suit coat. It was only nine A.M. "That's it," he said. "I'm through. Fifty years in the food business." I hadn't dreamed that the sight of Matilda in my wife's nightgown would do that to him. I'd just sent one of the world's finest butchers into retirement.

∽∽∽∽∽∽∽∽∽∽∽∽∽

Anyone can live off the land. There are roots and barks, even vegetable gardens, aplenty. But some wild foods are hardly worth the bother. Take dandelion jelly: "Gather only the bright yellow parts of the flower. Boil a quart of petals [fancy how long it takes to fill a quart container without getting a trace of green] in a quart of water for three minutes. Strain [yes indeed!] to get three cups of juice. Add one teaspoon of lemon extract, one package of pectin. Boil and add 4½ cups of sugar. Boil down and you'll end up with a delectable golden jelly called captured sunshine." Now who wants to go to all that trouble when he can fry up some day lily fritters instead? As I said, you're welcome to some wild cherry wine, or vinegar. We've more than enough to put on our poke sallet.

~~~~~~~~~~~~~~~~~~~~~~~~~~~~~~

Fishing supposedly slacks off by late June or early July, but the increase in Spanish mackerel has altered the old outlook. Charter boats on the waterfront are loading up with the sleek racers, and it looks as if it's going to be one of those great mackerel years. Not wanting to miss a potential bonanza, we were up early enough to see the sun just lifting out of the ocean, sending a broad red streak across the water to where we were cruising at mackerel speed in the shoal waters west of the inlet. We were dragging all manner of enticing hardware when a hovering of gulls pulled us into a circle and the action began.

There are many approaches to fishing, among them fishing for numbers and fishing for fun. I prefer to fish for fun, but this one time, even sorry angler that I am, the fish wouldn't let me quit. It would have been dangerous to dangle a finger close to the water, and a barb on the hook wasn't really necessary. Mary swore she could have held a lure above the fish box and iced the fish as they jumped in. Fishing like that doesn't occur very often. Though there was some argument over the actual numbers, we—three of us—boated between one and two hundred Spaniards and were back at the pier in time for a nine o'clock appointment. Another angler, one who thinks he knows fishing, came in after lunch with nary a scale, swearing he'd fished nearly to Bermuda and back. It didn't seem right to tell him of our skill. It's luck, you know, if the other fellow catches them, skill if you do.

Later we were discussing the sport at a waterfront coffee stop, and the talk became downright intellectual: which is the smartest fish of all? Of several nominations, billfish and mackerels weren't even in the running. The red snapper was named, for it tests the bait before chomping down, and can mull it over and still spit it out. Another nominee was the triggerfish, but all agreed that the most cunning and suspicious is the sheepshead, the fish so elusive that you must set the hook before it bites. It turned out that the unanimous winner for smarts was the jumping mullet. It seldom runs into a net it can see. Many a school surrounded by a net avoids capture simply by leaping over the net line. They are rarely caught on a hook, and pier fishermen have seen repeatedly how they move along the beach in a school, halting when they see a pier. They mill around as if in conference, then break up into small pods and slip around the pilings, regrouping on the other side. Right now, early as it is, we can see schools of tiny mullet in the inside waters practicing their maneuvers, getting ready for fall graduation.

PINK CLOUDS

*During the Thunder Moon the heated, hazy afternoon humidity
reflects the last rays of the sun. It's a time to dream, a period of
quick-passing thunderstorms. It's when those who dwell in warmer
regions most appreciate the coast.*

Midsummer brings on a few activities that seem downright strenuous. One of them is the Fourth of July,
which we celebrate with vigor morning and evening, with a
long rest between. It takes the whole family and several
neighbors to do it right. First, the night before, Mary alerts
the nearest neighbors that we will be celebrating. Next
morning, well before eight, my brother and I carry the Lyle
gun down to the shore. Its original purpose was to fire a line
to grounded ships in the days of the old Lifesaving Service.
Its caliber is the same as that of a hairspray can. Usually I
have measured powder and prepared primers the night before. The coign sets the trajectory to the middle of where
the creek makes into a little bay. A measure of blasting powder is put down the barrel first, followed by well-tamped, wet
newspapers. Then the primer and finally the firing mechanism are inserted and a long halyard attached.

Meanwhile, Mary has placed Sousa's "Under the Double
Eagle" on the stereo and opened all the windows, and Bill
has prepared to make morning colors: on the Fourth, a flag

with 13 stars. Seconds before eight my sister-in-law Susan, from her station on board *Sylvia II*, blows the danger signal for passing boats—four resounding "Ahhhoogas"—and stands by to raise the ship's colors.

At 0800—eight bells, you lubbers—Mary rings the bronze ship's bell that we kept from *Silver Spray* and rushes indoors to turn on the stereo. The cannon is fired, the flags go up and the neighbors get up. Within minutes our neighbor across the bay, John McGregor, fires his impudent little cannon back at us.

Those unfortunates who have never had the mad pleasure of firing a cannon have missed an important segment of life. To make an adequate comparison, think first of how much noise a twelve-gauge shotgun can make; then realize that the load of a three-inch magnum is a scant thimbleful of powder. Now, to load this bronze cannon, we start with a four- to six-ounce Dixie cup of No. 1 blasting grade black powder. The recoil is usually sufficient to send this 120-plus-pound mass of metal on its oak carriage sliding back twelve to fifteen feet, leaving a trail of torn turf.

It is no crack or bang. It is a ground-shuddering, window-rattling "BALOOOOM" that sets dogs to howling or kiyiping for cover. Leaves and branches fall, young and old people dance, and ducks fly. The load of wet, tamped newspapers is propelled by a ten- to twelve-foot shaft of flame into minute bits of smoking confetti, and followed by an immense toadstool of gray-white smoke that on a still day will set fog bells to ringing and blot out whole neighborhoods. Once and only once did we put a projectile in the cannon—a sand-filled Pepsi bottle that, when fired down an endless sea, was last seen skipping waves off towards Bermuda.

As the smoke clears and the reverberations die, and the flag goes up to that most exuberant of Sousa marches, for a minute or two we stand proudly watching it flap, and we feel good. Call us old-fashioned or immature, say that patriotism is out of style, that fireworks should be banned because fools like us might get hurt, say that speeches are boring and picnics draw flies. But I hope that we never lose that sense of pride.

Quite a few friends have helped us celebrate in the past, and come the next Fourth of July the neighbors will be wakened and hear the Marine Band playing that rousing Sousa march and see the flag snapping in the breeze at Simpson's Point Landing. There will be lemonade in the shade of the big oak tree, and more than one firing of the sundown cannon, because sometimes it's hard to get the sun to set.

〰〰〰〰〰〰〰〰〰〰〰

Will Rogers once said he never knew a man he didn't like. I guess that I feel the same way, except for one or two I may have some doubts about. But maybe it's because I don't really know them. It's a fact, though, that I do like some better than others. Take my friend Jim Dean, who came by one day accompanied by his young son. Jim was busy, while acting leisurely, teaching his kid "messin'." I wondered why he'd brought him to us, but then figured it wasn't personal. He was teaching his boy an art that is nearly lost in this hurly-burly world.

Why, there was a day when every town had a whittlers' bench, usually in the shade of an old oak, where fellows just whittled all day. Shavings up to their knees, long thin shavings or short thin shavings, but never a thick one in the lot, because those fellows weren't on a production line. They could make a stick of wood last all day. Their long, leaf-thin knife blades were worn near to the hilt and sharp as a razor. Red cedar was the favorite wood by far, and to the best of my recollection there wasn't a useful thing ever carved. Just messin'.

Messin' consists of things like sitting under a tree and looking, maybe braiding blades of grass, or counting a flight of birds. Serious ones might try to estimate the number of leaves in a tree, while the serious and lazy might only estimate the number of branches. But there is a real potential for danger here, like that fellow who got hit by a falling apple and figured out gravity. It ruined his days of messin' when he got serious. Many another good man has been lost to too-serious messin'.

One of the safest methods of messin' is wandering down a country road. Not too fast, as that comes under the category of hiking or even walking. Messin' is when one takes time to kick every tenth stone or so, watch a honey bee work over a flower, or practice answering a bobwhite. Boats are the very best area for messin', provided one doesn't go anywhere in particular, for the cardinal rule for success in the field is, Don't accomplish anything. It is wonderfully gratifying to the mind, and I must commend a father who will take his little son by the hand, go forth in the world and teach him the art and philosophy, unattainable in any known institute of public learning, of messin'.

True, it is like alcohol: taken in too large and frequent quantities over a long period, it may affect one's attitude towards the Puritan work ethic and cause great non-puritanical joy. The contemplation required for messin' can usually be covered up by pretending to be thinking, in case one happens to be caught by a member of society. Why doesn't the theory work when my wife catches me messin'?

Work itself can be a disease. Acute, insatiable appetites are the most visible symptoms, and a tendency to attach the stigma of "indolent" or "reactionary" to anyone not similarly fired with enthusiasm. Actually, the problem of those so afflicted is their lack of self-restraint, a quality almost unknown in the more successful and aggressive. These persons, caught in their own trap, are seldom happy. They have no time to enjoy the good life, much less recognize it.

Take the two friends on safari. They had spent several weeks of frenzied activity preparing for the trip of a lifetime. And it had been great to camp on the veldt, watch the vast herds of wild game migrate across the limitless land, fish the streams loaded with giant fish, sit around the campfire in the evening and see a red moon rising above a distant range of snow-topped mountains, hear the soft calls of flights of waterfowl passing overhead, and have native cooks prepare wondrous dishes of local foods.

They had experienced the finest in excitement, scenery, food, and company, but their time was up and they must return to the States, back to the office and jangling telephones, decisions, harassment, the old cutthroat routine, strangling stifling traffic, and the stench of the city. As they were bemoaning their fate on the way to the airport, they passed through a native village. There barebreasted women tended the gardens while the menfolks sat under a tree smoking their pipes and watching as the women waited on them. One of the hunters commented, "It must be hell to live like that." The native driver of the Land Rover smiled and drove on.

〰〰〰〰〰〰〰〰〰〰〰〰〰

Commercial fishermen either are very wealthy, have unlimited credit, or know something I don't know. For years I've watched neighbors and friends take their boats out, just before dusk, and come back next morning with baskets and boxes of shrimp. Because shrimp sells for around four dollars a pound, and they usually had several pounds of same, for which they had an immediate sale, it made me think that there must be something to the game. The other part suits me, too: whenever I saw them during the day, they were idling around under the trees, talking to their dogs, mending nets, fussing about the boats, or just cooling.

It seemed a good idea. All one needs is a net and a boat to pull it with, I thought. I already had *Sylvia II*, so I ordered a net. But there is more to nets than just a mess of string. There are purse nets, gill nets and haul nets, trawl nets, balloon nets, and throw nets, to mention but a few. The logical second step is to go to an expert and have one made. He will do this if you can explain what you intend to do. Lonnie Pittsman understood, and made one to order. Net making is a skill, and watching a man knit a net with both hands and (bare) feet is something to remember. There are those, of course, who can knit or mend a net with their shoes on.

The finished net was beautiful: yellow lines and black net with white trim and proper chains. I was ready. "Got your boards?" asked Lonnie. This was the first setback. Boards cost almost as much as a net, and nets cost by the foot, squaring in cost for every added foot. Still, fishermen do have the life. Like wealthy yachtsmen, all they do is run around in their boats all day, or night, or both. Why, just last week, flying over the sounds, we counted 105 boats, all fishing happily together. It looked like jolly good fun. Cap'n Frank Bayer watched as we rigged up. "Where's a good place to try it out?" we asked. "Well, might try the south channel, but watch for the snag by the villa, just past the channel marker." We were impatient to start and eager to let *Sylvia II* earn her keep.

Dusk was settling over the sound, and the last of the sea birds were winging in through violet darkness to gather, white against black, on little islands awash with small phosphorescent waves. Distant lights blinked far down the sound, marking the Waterways. Homes, snuggled against the bluffs, glowed warmly. The stars were coming out.

Trawling is great sport. When one lets out the net, careful-like so's not to tangle it, there is a game of skip the rope, or how to avoid having a leg snatched off quick and drowning at the same time. When net meets water, even with the boat barely moving, all those ropes and lines can tangle and grab at almost anything. Dominant was the slow rumble of the engine straining against the net as it slid along the bottom. Only the float marking the tail bag could be seen, bobbing and twirling. About us, red and green running lights of other boats looked like jewels, and the trawling lights floated moonlike atop the masts.

Slowly, against an ebbing tide, *Sylvia II* churned on, water phosphorescing from the wheel's stirring and where the trawl lines slashed. The radium hands of the clock moved as the stars overhead, imperceptibly but surely. The first haul emerged as a greenish ghost. Eager hands hoisted the net aboard and, by pale lantern light, untied the bag to let the contents cascade across the deck.

There were flipping fish; scuttling crabs waving claws defiantly; spiny urchins purple and glistening, their quills moving sluggishly; sea whips and beer cans, pulsating jellyfish and gobs of protoplasm; squid, and the real goal—shrimp, big, fat, and brown, with fiery eyes and snapping tails. We sorted the catch: six shrimp, eight squid. Crabs and fish, most too small to keep, were scraped quickly overboard. We were proud, but just slightly disappointed at the take.

The bag retied, we eased the net over the stern and resumed our patrol.

The light westerly breeze freshened, with a few whitecaps. The rigging sang in soft voices. It wasn't long, though, before the shore-line ceased to drift by. Curious, we looked about. The trawl lines seemed uncommonly tight. Mary closed the throttle, *Sylvia II* pulled back against the sloppy chop and hung, securely anchored by a snag. The wind increased. The waves increased. No longer did it seem so romantic. Tugging and twisting were to no avail. We could cut the lines and lose a trawl, or spend the night and see what morning would bring. But Mary came up with two bleach jugs to tie to the line. We attached a light from the life ring, and it showed alter-nately white and yellow-green as it dipped into the waves. We headed home.

Ashore, Cap'n Frank remarked, "Oh, that snag! Thought everyone knew about that. That ain't the 'villa snag'." As I said, fishermen are wealthy, have good credit, or know something I don't know. By my reckoning, those few shrimp ran about $3,654.00 a pound, dressed. At the rate I fish, it might be cheaper to patronize the local market, says John Weeks the fish dealer.

Intimidated—that's the way you feel when you are overwhelmed by another's superior fishing skill or other talent. I was sitting on the bow of *Sylvia II*, messin', of course. You know what I mean if you understand boats. There was this crack in the paint, and the wood was a bit damp, so I carefully scraped away the finish to let the wood dry before touching up with a bit of putty and paint.

It was a weekend, and a stream of boats was going by. From one of those plastic jobs "Mac" McDonald needled, "Gee, I wish I had a wooden boat so I could work on it all the time!" Another fellow yelled across the intervening water, "Hey Bob! Don't you ever go out?" and he held up a nice fat king, must have been a thirty-pounder. I waved back, murmuring some wise remark, very much aware that I was tied up and he wasn't. Seeking to drown my sorrows, I took a break and headed for the local coffee emporium.

Reveling in air-conditioned relief, I heard two voices from a table behind me. "Yeah man! I got a big one, a blue. It weighed right at 230." The other voice replied, "We raised a couple. Two strikes just beyond the Big Rock." The coffee no longer had the bouquet and flavor of a few moments before. I went home and twisted knobs on the TV set—maybe Franc White, the Southern Sportsman, would have a program to cheer me up.

Sure enough, there on the tube flicked the likeness of Franc, grinning like a mule eating briars—and holding up this ten- or twenty-pound trout. His wife Lee then hoisted a bigger one, modestly admitting that she'd caught maybe ten. It might as well have been twenty, and it all seemed so simple. Their boat was "near 'bout" swamped with fish, and I couldn't remember ever catching a trout over two or three pounds. I was lower than a grasshopper's belly as I slumped into the sofa with a bowl of popcorn and an iced drink. Munching and sipping and watching those two catch fish, I did my best to figure it out.

Finally it came to me. There are the doers and the messers. There are those folks who go out and stand on the mountaintop while looking for a bigger one to climb. There are those who catch only the biggest fish, chase the fastest women, or make nothing less than millions every time they move. Then there are the rest of us, the messers, who can't seem to get that ambitious. Oh, we may have a flash of glory now and then in the form of a three-pound bass, but most of the time we are happiest just messin'.

I've been marlin fishing and, frankly, I find it a bit of a bore, with only occasional moments of excitement. Yet I can take *Sylvia II* and go poking around back creeks and bays, exploring sloughs and canals, and have a great time. There are also the happy hours spent swinging in a hammock, making analytical studies of birds, squirrels, and clouds. And casting a plug is just fine, if the fish want to bite. But I can get almost as much fun out of just moseying down a lazy creek with a dragonfly to keep me company, so why should I feel intimidated?

So far, I have had no desire for a forty-, fifty- or hundred-knot boat, any more than I yearn for a DC-10 or a 747. The Old Town canoe is more my class, although I'll admit I've looked with great admiration on the pedal-powered flying machine the fellow flew across the English Channel. Even though I doubt it would solve my transportation problems, it's pretty neat. As for boats, there are the fishing machines, the hurrying machines, and those for messing about. Can you imagine one of those chrome-plated and teak jobs with a hammock slung between fighting chair and gin pole and a canvas awning lashed to the outriggers, at anchor in the Hook of the Cape while the owner dips a hook for pinfish?

Nope, those fellows, poor souls, have a reputation to live up to, and couldn't be seen baiting up to catch a sea mullet or gunkholing in some remote backwater. They are stuck with big fish they can't eat, while we messers—well, as long as we don't expect anything, we are seldom disappointed. So, when you see an achiever, coming into view, you should not cower in the bilges, nor merge with the merkle bushes, but remember that messers are the ones who initiated great moments in history like jumping frog contests, cockroach racing, crab derbies, and hawg callin's.

~~~~~~~~~~~~~~~~~~~~~~

A long time ago we were living in Florida on our first boat, the yacht *Silver Spray*, which some folks might not think of as a yacht, but we did. She was a bit old and rough, and her seams showed, but to us she was a yacht. I was a serious young man, seeking that great All-American goal of success and money, though not necessarily in that order. I, too, was going to set the world on fire. Then, one weekend in the Keys, I met this fellow from North Carolina, sallow-faced, with dark, intense eyes and a bright orange-red beard.

Every now and then I think about him and his homemade sloop, not much of a boat, built in a backyard by unskilled hands. Squarish, tubby, patched together, it floated, maybe not very well; but at least when I saw it, it was bobbing alongside the fuel dock to the chagrin of the dockmaster. Chagrin comes easy to a dockmaster who recognizes a boat that never takes on fuel.

There was no name on the transom. "Where're you heading?" I asked.

"Not sure. South, Cuba, maybe."

It was a friendly Cuba then. He had no compass that I could see, nor were any navigational charts in evidence. How then could he navigate? He pointed to a cloud on the southern horizon. The pinkish-gold rays of the sun setting behind a calm sea tinted the underside of the cloud. "I'll follow that cloud." I edged away. Here he was, college and all, parents outstanding educators, and he was going to follow a wispy cloud? The guy must've lost a few marbles along the way, I thought, pragmatist that I considered myself in those days.

For many years that memory kept bugging me, as I began to realize that maybe I, too, wasn't cut out for this success bit. It seemed to involve a kind of single-mindedness that didn't suit me. Maybe that chap was onto something I didn't understand. A dreamer? A yearner? Perhaps it was simply as Thoreau had put it: he was in step with a different drummer. His ideals and goals were different, but no less valid.

My red-bearded friend had set sail, of course, and I heard later that he'd wrecked farther down the coast. Kindly people rescued him, fed him and helped him on his way. Surely they felt better for helping, and there is little doubt that he gave them something besides golf and the stock market to talk about, good or bad. He provided them a thrill, as he undoubtedly did when Cubans found him in difficulty on a shoal off their coast a few weeks later. They guided him to harbor; he regaled them with his tales. They listened in wonder at the carrot-bearded one, and thought new thoughts. He added spice to their lives, and they to his.

Dreamers are the impractical ones. But it is they who provide excitement and fresh ideas. When Columbus set sail, he wasn't being practical; he was a dreamer. It just happened that his dream turned out somewhat differently from the original plan. But each reliable, dependable person on earth should have a go at a large adventure, too. A full-time adventurer, professional or amateur, should not have exclusive rights to all the big thrills. My wife, who gets hopelessly seasick, greatly admires the fellow who worked on a newspaper, the Cleveland *Plain Dealer* as I recall, and who, one day after about fifteen years at the copy desk, decided that if he was really going to make his dream come true, he had better get at it. So he set sail single-handed across the Atlantic in a tiny boat named *Tinker Bell*, though he'd never been to sea before. He made it. If he hadn't he'd have been called a stupid fool, but he did, and, though perhaps still a hero-type fool, he'd proved to himself that he was alive. A good friend of mine once tried via outboard to get to Bermuda. He didn't make it, but he gave it all he had.

So leave room for the dreamers. Some are seeking Utopia, others simply to escape. Some will never even try; others will make a supreme effort against heavy odds. And then there's the matter of age. I once worked for a very successful and wealthy man. On the flybridge of his yacht one day he turned to me and said, "All my life I've worked hard to get to be wealthy enough to do all the things I've found only a young man can enjoy."

Find a goal in life and go after it, I was told. But that goal is sometimes elusive, and heading too directly for it might cause one to miss the scenery along the way. Take the interstate highway system: the sole objective is to get you somewhere. It does a remarkable job, something like going by jet, but man! it's a dull trip. From an interstate we seldom get to see the real world. Take a back road. It lets you drive past farmyards and cornfields and maybe there'll be a fruit stand along the way. Back roads lead into little villages with dusty old stores and folks sitting on the porches who'll wave at you. Perhaps a real, honest-to-God Mom and Pop's restaurant will serve you genuine homemade pies and sweet rolls, not the pre-packaged mass-mixed monotony. Airlines? If you are in a hurry, a jet will surely get there that way, and you'll see little or nothing. Zip, bang, and pick up your luggage from the conveyor.

Now the last time I took a train ride, it was actually going no-where, but it is one of my most idyllic memories. We left Cochrane, Ontario, headed north on the Polar Bear Express. No seat belts, everyone wandered around visiting and getting acquainted. There was the fellow with the mouth organ, who challenged the man with the squeezebox, and how the music rolled out! Passengers sang old-time songs that were old-time when their parents were kids, and stomped their feet. In the dining car hamburgers and soup and pie were the best I'd had in a long time, and the girls at the counter were just as pretty as any airline stewardess, and didn't wear uniforms. Even though the trip was long in hours, it wasn't short in the things that counted.

It seems that the more efficient, the less fun. Not long ago I took a nonstop jet to the west coast. Efficient. A few years earlier I'd gone west by light plane; there were three of us. Sure, by jet we did it in a quarter of a day, while the small aircraft, a stem winder, took three days. We'd watch the sun chase us across the Appalachians as we winged over those dark green mountains to stop in a forgotten little airport in Tennessee for fuel. We visited with other wanderers. We watched the Mississippi meander, all bright and silvery, studied the cornfields of Iowa, and descended with the sun in Kansas City. After the wheat fields we met the rising Rockies emerging from the Great Plains and spent the night in Cheyenne. That flight I'll never forget. The jet? Just another wham, bam, thank you ma'am.

The art of travel? Well, lots of words have been written about it, but the art is in the traveling, not in getting there. To take a horse and head for a distant mountain, or a sailboat and follow a pink cloud, that is the joy, not picking up your bags from the endless belt at the airline terminal.

DOG DAYS

*Autumn is straining to happen as early as August, just as winter
shows fat sassafras buds almost as soon as the leaves fall. Dog
days occur roughly between mid-July and mid-September, when
the Dog Star Sirius is in conjunction with our sun.*

Whenever the ice in my drink runs low, I get to dreaming of snow-topped peaks and cooling glaciers. The hammock no longer seems supportive, and the shade of the live
oak is oppressive. Re-iced, I begin to appreciate that no place
has a monopoly on beauty. And then I go out to renew
acquaintance with the byways to which *Sylvia II* takes me.
How had I overlooked the symmetry of a tide-swept sand flat,
the powder blue of sky and the puffy clouds building to the
west? How had I missed the creamy white of scoured sand,
wave-rippled, that extends towards that distant island? Or the
bright yellow-green of summer marshes, wild horses standing
ankle deep in the afternoon sun, a yearling colt napping on the
beach? Or the twisting, turning channels of blue and green
waters and the swirling balls of seaweeds, a tumble of reds and
greens and grays that rushes with the incoming tide?

As if for the first time, I watch the scampering sandpipers skirting the water's edge, pausing to poke their stiletto bills into the sand. Gulls rest on the ridges, facing the light breeze. A great ship, the storm-cloud gray of war, pushes a bow wave as it steams toward some distant port. Sand dollars lie buried in sand and mud, to be found by feeling with the fingers, only one's head above the warm, salty waters. Colonies of periwinkles are scattered across the mucky shallows. Watching the clouds slide by, I feel wrapped in complacency, and not until the sun falls behind the horizon in a glorious blaze can I admit that all good things must end, so that other good things can take their place.

Pipe dreams are easy enough to come by when you're swinging comfortably in a hammock, and only occasionally do they lead to something practical. Our earlier idle talk about the future of *Sylvia II* had been just that, but the seed had been planted. For a long time we had been writing articles in the vein of improving readers' understanding of the water, of the interrelationship of landsman, fish and fisherman, hoping that perhaps it would lead to more interest in the protection of marine resources. Now I'm well aware that such enlightenment can work in reverse. In the 1940s and even into the 1950s no one seemed to give a damn about the beaches except as places to visit now and then. The ideal at that time was not to have a second or third home on a sand dune. No, a visit to the ocean consisted of staying a day or so at a resort village, maybe chartering a boat for a fishing expedition. Then as people became more affluent, they began to expect not only a second or third home—one on the beach, perhaps another in the mountains—but to own a boat, too. As a result, the beaches are, to a considerable extent, ravished beauties. It's almost as if we'd built a housing complex in a redwood forest: the forest has somehow lost its charm.

At any rate, the idea of chartering *Sylvia II* appealed to us. We wanted to share the fun, yes, but we wanted, too, to show landsmen why we consider the estuarine areas as they are now so important, so valuable. We could have gone the usual route of putting on a pair of trolling rods and engaged in chasing bluefish and mackerel; but waterfront charterboats were already doing this, so we devised the educational charter service, catering to family and school groups.

Our commercial fishing sampler goes like this: the previous evening we plant a half-dozen crab pots and a gill net or two in the sound, out of the traffic, but close enough to port so that our charter parties are doing something within minutes of boarding. Next morning at eight the party boards and we give them a brief safety talk before firing up the engine and casting off. Once out of the channel we start picking up crab pots. My brother Bill, acting as mate, stands guard on the weather deck, seeing to the safety of the passengers. I run the boat and the party does the work. It's something like a dude ranch where people pay to feed the horses.

We proceed then to the nets, which the party helps haul aboard along with their contents, if any. After that we drop a trawl over the stern and make two or three fifteen-minute sweeps, picking up clam shells, seaweed, beer cans, once in a while a seahorse, fish or squid, perhaps a shrimp or two. Meanwhile, there's explanation of how to tell a she-crab from a jimmy and identification of the whole grab bag of marine life. After the first two hours, we nose *Sylvia II* up to the shoals, send the party ashore by skiff or wading with clam rakes, buckets, and minnow nets. There, on one of a series of small dredge islands, they try to find a clam or a conch and splash in the water. Around noon we round them up, pick up the crab pots, and return them to the dock, happy, tired, even a little sunburned. We always inform them that for fish or other seafood the fish market is cheaper and more dependable, that they are not supposed to catch a meal, but samples.

Gradually discovered by several schools in and out of state, *Sylvia II* has taken many teachers, high school and college students for educational cruises. As time goes on, it has become more important to talk a prospective party out of a trip than into one, for while chartering is lots of fun, it involves time and work and interferes with play. Other people with boats have tried similar services, but most were more interested in huge catches than in having fun, or else unaware of one essential item, licensing: a commercial license and a Coast Guard license are required. The state commercial license is simply a matter of money, but to obtain a Coast Guard license to carry passengers for hire gets to be right tough.

It's not that the Coast Guard gives anyone a hard time; it simply insists that you know what you're doing. Lest anyone think that a license isn't hard to get, consider that it takes about 250 hours of flight time to obtain a license to fly a commercial jet, while it takes a certified year of actual experience before you can even apply for your first license on a boat. A tugboat captain tells me that it takes 2,080 hours' experience before one can apply for a mate's license, after which one must go for an exam that includes first aid, rules of the road, international and inland, oil spills, navigation, fire fighting, safety, and more.

This is not to be construed as suggesting that every boatman be licensed. Licensing at present applies only to operating a boat of any size carrying passengers for hire, and for operating commercial craft like tugs, ferries, and large ships. There has never been a fatal accident among the skippers of the Morehead City charter fleet. Yet every season the crews help in rescuing some novice who heads to sea in a craft unsuitable for offshore cruising or who does not know what he is doing. The watermen's sentiment is that while you have the right to be a fool, if you are a professional you don't go beyond your capabilities and endanger others.

Any boat operator, with or without a license, is responsible for handling his boat safely, and groups like the Coast Guard Auxiliary and the Power Squadron offer boating safety courses to the public. The waterways are the last refuge of the free soul, who can take out his log, raft, or skiff and paddle down the sound without having to ask anyone's permission.

I feel confident that *Sylvia II* has helped teachers and students alike to appreciate that the bodies of water so many of us consider only an excuse for water-skiing or waterfront construction have a greater purpose and a value worth our keeping them as near to pristine as possible.

The first moon after the longest day, said the ancients, is the Moon of the Yellow Fly. Knowing this, but also aware that the bass in the Trent River were reportedly big, we put aboard our canoe, life jackets, and such, and set out for the rich bass mine. The stream was beautiful, but we had scarcely parked the car and begun unloading gear before the first attack came. We could visualize their smelling the insect repellent and rubbing their legs together in gleeful anticipation of another luncheon of fresh two-legs. On the stream it was worse. We needed no more reminders that it is indeed the Moon of the Yellow Fly.

But offshore, where a canopy of towering clouds is forming bastions above the Gulf Stream, and where there are no yellow flies, flying fish are spreading their wide, transparent pectoral fins and bursting out of the quiet security of their natural home to skip like happy children through the strange and exciting medium known as the atmosphere. They bounce from wave to wave until they have to dive deep and refresh their aching gills in the cool brine.

On the far horizon a freighter plods its way north towards Cape Hatteras, only the bulk of its superstructure visible above the undulating seas. And inshore, just above the water, a flight of gulls hovers, alternately wheeling, swooping, and plummeting onto the disturbed surface where a school of Spanish mackerel is pursuing small bait fish; they leap into the air in a frantic effort to escape, only to be seized by waiting gull above or fish below.

For the next two months the only fit place to be on the coast will be in a boat, seeking the open sounds and offshore breezes. This may explain the abundance of high seas adventure stories that make their way ashore at this time of year, such as this one: eight miles from nearest land the little sailer hove into sight across the infinity of ocean, a mere speck at first, too insignificant to be measured in normal terms. Sails set, it glided on. A passing sportsfisherman on a long offshore trip spotted it, but could see no one aboard. Cruising alongside, he still saw no sign of life. Closing in, he sounded the horn. A hatch snapped open, a head emerged and a young man came scrambling out. "Got a quart of oil?" Days, weeks out of the Bahamas, single-handed in the shipping lanes, he had his little eighteen-footer dead on course, bound for Morehead City from Nassau, twelve hundred miles alone across a trackless, watery wilderness. It takes a special breed.

Under the same Yellow Fly Moon, the sultry summer haze lay over the land, softening the distant horizon, muting the blushing sky. The sun was reflected in a band of rippled red across the sound. *Sylvia II* swayed on her anchorline in the changing tide, the water muttering around her. While our dinner cooked on a little island, we swam in the warm, soothing water that flowed on across the sculptured sand flats in the last of the ebb. A sailboat, aground, sat solidly nearby, its coppered bottom exposed. The crew lounged in the cockpit, smoking and talking in quiet tones as they waited patiently for the next tide to float them free in a few hours.

Oystercatchers, strange leggy birds with knobby orange bills, uttered harsh and angry sounds as they flew low to settle on the spoil bank where they had recently reared their young. Standing on the shelly beach, they watched us as if they were still proprietors. The charcoal grill was putting out the smoky odors of hamburgers sizzling. The light breeze carried the aroma towards the grounded boat, but the crew chose to ignore the tantalizing scents. Coming out of the water, I paused to watch the birds stalking the shallows in the last of the fading light. A small crab scuttled across my toes, stirring up puffs of mud and sand.

I wondered how much longer there would be such privacy and isolation for today's youth, how much wilderness. Coming back to me were the words of Clinton Anderson, former Secretary of Agriculture, a hard-headed businessman who believed in our economic system: "Wilderness is an anchor to windward. Knowing it is there, we can also know we are still a rich nation, tending to our resources as we should. Not as a people in desperation, scratching every last nook and cranny of our land for a board of lumber, a barrel of oil, a blade of grass or a tank of water." When people talk of wilderness, they most often think of great snow-capped mountains and deep, dark valleys, of lonely eagles and endless blue skies. But there are other wildernesses: there are bottomless bogs and dense pocosins such as Okefenokee and the Great Dismal Swamp, homes of wood storks and alligators, of bears and panthers. There is the canoe country of the North, rocky waterways in jack pine land where loon and wolf still send laughter and howl echoing across silent lands and waters.

And too few people think of the back rivers, of the little bays and estuaries, as parts of our real wilderness system. Not formally designated, not even legally recognized, they are still equally—perhaps even more—valuable to man, besides being more accessible than what we commonly think of as wilderness. Our educational system has failed badly in its obligation to teach such real values, while the advertising industry has done a superb job of indoctrinating us in false values. Within our economic system, admen have convinced many of us of the validity of these standards. Successfully, we have been taught that Scotch whiskey and caviar, not home-brew and mullet roe, are the ultimate, for we have learned to esteem price. Too few of us have found that water slakes thirst as well as the more expensive substitutes, without some of the side effects. So it is with wilderness, because many cannot find a value in anything unless it's paved and costly.

The pearly grayness of dusk faded to black. Overhead the Big Dipper handle stood pointing to the southern sky, its summer stance. Gradually it would swing more and more to the west, and a new season would replace summer. Perhaps in the long history of the earth it doesn't matter, as archaeologists uncover the remains of our systems in a few thousand years. Will they laugh, or will they wish that they, too, could have lived in this century? It depends mainly on us, and which philosophy we express when we refer to GNP. Do we mean Gross National Product or Glacier National Park?

~~~~~~~~~~~~~~~~~~~~~~~~

Floundering is an adventure, no matter how often it is done. There are few persons with souls so dead that they will not jump at an opportunity to stalk the Carolina flatfish, the only fish truly designed to fit a fry pan. Floundering is equal parts gamble and science. I've known commercial fishermen to boat more than a ton in a night—that's two men with gigs—or come home skunked. These fish run from a pound or so to well over fifteen pounds, and I can personally testify to eleven pounds, which is huge for a flounder, though small for a halibut. Halibut gigging, I understand, is not common.

Floundering is also something you can do to entertain the jaded recreational appetites of visitors. One summer we found ourselves with guests from California on their first trip to the South, the Deep South. From the land of milk and honey, they expected to find the quaint little fishing village on the Carolina beaches a bit dull. Still, they were curious enough to come, so we undertook to entertain them in the way we knew best, beginning with what in the Marine Corps we used to call a Snow Job.

My briefing before this nighttime foray into the marine world required categorizing of the life to be found therein—roughly, three classifications: (1) flounder; (2) skates, rays, and torpedoes; and (3) anything else, such as squid, octopi, crabs, conchs, eels, and varmints. To distinguish among them and avoid calamitous errors, one should know the basic differences.

A flounder is a somewhat oval-shaped ("ovate," as we say in the trade) flatfish that lies on its side on the bottom. No Marine, no duck hunter ever had better camouflage. Simulating the colors and patterns of the bottom, it shudders a bit, covering itself lightly with sand, and only its eyes, both on the same side of its head, are revealed. Rippled or murky water makes it invisible to the untrained eye.

Skates, rays, torpedoes, and the rest are what one should look out for. Skates, rays, and torpedoes are more diamond-shaped, but also invisible to the unobservant, and get rather larger than a flounder. A manta ray, for example, may be as much as twenty-two feet across. It is recommended that one not gig them. If yielding to the temptation, it is best to plant the gig rather deeply between the eyes, for they have been known to exceed twenty knots, weigh up to 3,000 pounds and clear reefs in a single leap. It is usually necessary to stand between the wings in order to gig effectively. This does add considerably to the excitement.

Coming down the scale, we find the common rays. The cow-nosed ray, though seldom over seven feet, can also provide more than adequate power for water skiing, besides a rather nasty barb in the tail area with which to gig the gigger. Then there are torpedoes, which could easily be confused with flounder, but there is a tingling difference. Gigging a torpedo is best described as like gigging an electric light socket. Its self-contained power pack is potent enough to make the unfortunate gigger flicker like a channel marker, in both red and green.

Skates are not unlike rays, but usually smaller, being rarely more than six feet long. They are milder in reaction, except, of course, when being gigged. I gigged a skate once, and I remember it well. This speckled fellow went swimming by and looked quite small. I planted the spear slightly forward of amidships, having about six feet of fairly stout cord wrapped once about my wrist to prevent loss of spear. It is still very clear to me: departing the rock jetty on which my feet had been firmly planted, and finding myself surfing along at, by my estimate, eight to ten knots on a south-southwesterly course. I'd covered eighty-five to a hundred yards before it occurred to me to let go. When last seen the tip of the handle was plowing a white furrow towards Trinidad.

Ah, but youth is restless, and these two wanted to experience floundering, not skating. It was well after dark and the waters were already black and mysterious when my brother Bill began pumping the Coleman kerosene lantern. The rhythmic click-click-click brought everyone outside. The lantern hissed to life, flooding the lawn with a white glow. Gigs, cushions, and a flashlight aboard, we shoved the skiff into the velvet warmth of the creek, to row slowly out the little inlet into the sound. The tide was still ebbing when we nosed the skiff ashore on a shelly beach and stepped out.

When we'd asked Susie and Zain if they would like to go floundering, Zain, raised in a small Malaysian village near the sea, was excited. Though fish was an important part of his diet, he was a landsman who knew little of fishing, especially at night. Susie, a typical young modern, had once fished a stocked California trout stream. Both were skeptical, walking slowly and quietly along the sandy shore in the dark, hearing the plaintive call of passing skimmers. This fishing must have seemed too much like a snipe hunt, if indeed they'd ever heard of a snipe hunt. It was quite a sight: darkness enfolding so that our entire world was within the pool of lantern light; hazy starlit sky, lantern flashes glinting off light ripples; explorers surging, knee deep, across muddy, sandy shoals, spears at the ready, guarding against spooks and goblins.

Our little troop splashed along. Insects and frogs could be heard ashore, above the hiss of the lantern. Dark shadows and shapes floated here and there—small fish sleeping beside barnacle-covered shells or amid the fronds of softly waving clumps of sea grasses. Needlefish, startled by the light, rushed about in confusion. Shrimp, eyes glowing a fierce, fiery red, lay in tiny holes and looked out, blinded by the light. An eel undulated slowly from a tangle of seaweed and slithered into a patch of eel grass flattened by the current. A rusted beer can, a glove buried in the sand, the mud-camouflaged outline of a bottle: these and other inescapable signs of humankind pass beneath the flounderer's light.

We moved slowly through the knee-deep shallows searching for the flounder's shadowy outline. Crabs scuttled sideways, then stopped, ready to take on all comers, waving their claws menacingly. But we were not looking for crabs, large as these were. Hermit crabs hurried out of our path, dragging their shells until we came too close, then disappearing completely into the shells. A sand dab shot away from us in ruffled flight.

"Now that's where our use of *dab* must have come from—not enough to be worth saving," and Mary went on about other flatfishes, the soles and turbots and halibuts. She conjectured about how to fillet a five-hundred-pounder and then remarked how well flatfishes' names lend themselves to puns. She pointed out a sole (of a shoe), which Bill gigged, just for the halibut. We waded on through the turbot water.

"There's one!" Ahead I'd finally spotted a suspicious-looking shape shifting slightly in the sand. A quick thrust of the gig just behind the head, and the bottom churned. The neophytes, startled, hadn't seen a thing. Reaching beneath the flounder, I flipped it into the skiff. The two studied the thrashing fish solemnly. They'd convinced themselves that this kind of fishing must be a big hoax, but now their interest brightened. Another flounder, a small one, showed the faintest outline in mud and sand. Two knobby eyes protruding were the only giveaway. Zain reached down to touch it. A puff of mud and it was gone. He roared with laughter. We ambled through the darkness in a magic world of our own.

A sudden splash and a squeal. I turned and here was this wisp of a girl hanging onto a spear and dancing in excitement. "I think I got one!" She sure had something and it was big. A few moments for the mud to settle, and the edge of a fin showed that Susie had a flounder. By this time our two dudes had been converted. Zain poked at a crab. The crab snapped back. This pleased him. Then the crab made a run in his direction. The hopping was mighty and excited. "It attacked me!" he announced in disbelief, almost accusingly. Then it was Susie's turn: "What's that?" she pointed.

"Crab."

She thought I said, "Grab!" and she did.

Fiery-eyed shrimp flicked their tails and disappeared when we came close. Conchs stalked the bottom. Venus had set long ago. The tide had turned. Lights from an approaching tug and barges glowed like monster eyes. The throb of diesel power rumbled. Long after the tow had passed, the wake could be felt, then heard as it slid ashore.

A few more flounder met their fate. The Big Dipper was leaning towards the western horizon. Haze had cut visibility short. The tide was well on its return when the bow of the skiff scraped on our shell landing. I stepped out and spooked the largest flounder we'd yet seen. We unloaded gear. The lantern, turned off, sighed and sputtered. A small blue flame glowed. A last flare and the light expired. Skiff well tied to a wild cherry tree and oars stowed, we returned to the silent house, cleaned and chilled the fish and toasted a night that the two—Westerner and Oriental—had discovered was no snipe hunt.

<hr />

Dog days come around this time of year, the transition of summer from youth to middle age. Like the first gray hairs, the signs are to be seen in an occasional leaf turned yellow, the flash of red sumac, "premature, of course." But there is much heat left, despite the sun's getting up a little later and setting a few minutes earlier. More than ten hours out of twenty-four are in darkness now, and their number is increasing. Dog days come when the star Vega is high overhead in early evening and the Dog Star, brightest in the heavens, is invisible, being in line with the sun. Vega is the summer star reaching its zenith when the sun has descended beyond the western fields.

My dog claims this as the Year of the Flea. Calendar says it's dog days, so she may be right. It is the time of year to philosophize, too, because it's hardly fit for anything else except fishing, swimming, and growing crops. The dog and I were working over this thought while reposing beneath the big live oak. A light sou'west breeze, damp and salty, was causing a slight swaying of the Spanish moss. Overhead, jays and squirrels were quarreling. The dog was eyeing a rabbit munching grass in the shade of a pecan, but she had no serious thoughts of chasing it, knowing full well that only "mad dogs and Englishmen go out in the noonday sun." Besides, it was taking all the energy she could muster just to scratch.

Dog days are the climax of the summer. The birds have completed their nesting. Ducks are in the moult. As the days shorten, still almost imperceptibly, the sultry heat becomes more intense, parching the earth, steaming the swamps, drying rivers and lakes. The heat drives out the oxygen, stagnating pools now surrounded by drying scum and baking mud. Then the heavens, unable to endure the earth's agony, flash in anger and darkness, to release the stored waters of life.

But women don't understand all these things, and the sight of an idle man or dog is offensive to them, somehow. They believe that idle men are just begging for something to do, like mowing the grass, hoeing the garden, or fixing something, anything. This, according to the great reasoner Robert Ruark, is why men go fishing. At least they are out of sight and contribute less to women's ire. But I'd forgotten this philosophy and was simply trying to be helpful, aiding my wife by giving her timely and constructive suggestions in homemaking. She had set up the Coleman camp stove in the shady backyard, on the upturned end of an old wire spool. On the fire was a great pot of bubbling, purple-foaming substance, and hard by, as writers of classic literature used to say, was a collection of old glass jars which she was filling with wild cherry jam.

Now I'd finished my work long before, and the keg of mashed cherries and sugar was working itself into a froth in the pumphouse. The difference is that man lets nature work for him, while women want to subdue it. I've often wondered why there are so few women engineers. To normal man, an eager beaver is just naturally suspect. I think it was about the time the pot boiled over that I felt it advisable to seek refuge in a quieter and more serene world. It was still too hot to fish, but I found an air-conditioned haven in the quiet halls of science and short-order cooking where I go to talk about fish.

⚬⚬⚬⚬⚬⚬⚬⚬⚬⚬⚬⚬⚬⚬

August, month of change, sees the first mass of cold air attempting to break through the dominating heat of summer, when lines of thunderstorms race across the heart of the nation. It is also the time in the doldrums when low pressure areas develop slowly, churning warm, moist tropical air into circulating wind patterns. Some grow into tropical disturbances, hardly noticed at first except by weather satellites. A few will grow into the most devastating type of storm—hurricane—meandering generally in a westerly direction until some atmospheric signal causes them to take up scarcely predictable courses, most often northerly. Down East Carolinians call northeast winds at this season mullet blows. Hurricanes are still referred to by old-timers as equinoctial storms.

This morning, early for me, though most of the boats had already cleared the docks, I was finishing the last cup of coffee at Sonny's on the waterfront when one of my favorite fishermen wandered in. "Fishing's lousy," was his greeting. "What we need—I hate to say it out loud—is a good hurricane to stir things up." Suddenly, in clearest recall, it was years ago and I was standing but a few yards away. The sky was black, the wind screaming and huge waves cascading in fury and incredible strength over the sea wall. A steam-powered dragline on a barge had sought the shelter of the low island called Sugarloaf in front of town. Only occasionally could we see flashes of it between deluges of wind-driven rain. Fire and sparks spouted from the stack as the crew maintained a peak head of steam in an attempt to hold its position through the night. We could hear, above the roar of the wind, clanking and splashing as the dragging anchors on the corners, weighing upwards of a ton, were heaved by the gargantuan crane and flung into the teeth of the storm. I don't remember that fishing picked up soon afterwards, because we had two more hurricanes within the next month.

After experiencing even one hurricane, one tends to become wary. In another storm—why always at night?—I was trying to get some news film. I edged my MG through hub-deep water, dodging debris of every sort. I saw, by the loom of the headlights, a whole roof whirling by. Like a giant frisbee, it had appeared out of the darkness, sailed just overhead, and disappeared into the night. By this time I was scarcely able to hold the car into the wind. Even in low gear it bounced and tossed. Then, in an explosion of canvas, the convertible top followed the flying roof, and I decided to forget about the news film.

I managed to get the car to high ground, opened the door to let the water run out and slogged towards the safety of *Silver Spray*. Moored in the most secure and sheltered of anchorages, she was like a beacon in the storm. All else—homes and shops nearby—was dark, with black waters swirling through broken windows. I waded cautiously to where the dinghy was tied, bailed it and rowed out to the boat. All the hurricanes we've experienced we've weathered aboard our boat in a snug hurricane harbor—and all the hurricane threats, too. When the National Weather Service says "Hoist hurricane warnings," we don't take it lightly. From a fisherman's point of view, a quick hurricane is better than a prolonged nor'easter, so we always see to the safety of our favorite rods and reels. After a series of devastating hurricanes in the fifties and sixties local people like to recall that, immediately following Hurricane Donna, the town board and Mayor Pat Dill passed an ordinance prohibiting hurricanes within the Morehead City limits, and there hasn't been another hurricane in town since.

∞∞∞∞∞∞∞∞∞∞∞∞∞∞∞∞

It seems just a short time ago that everyone was going around telling one another how they loved hot weather. Now that they've had a good dose of it, one doesn't hear much from them. Even the cicada started out right noisy in praise of the first hot day, rubbing its belly with enthusiasm, but it, too, has a somewhat threadbare sound. Summer is a necessary evil: time to grow food, our last chance until the next planting. It's too hot to work, so one tries for the least activity, from shade to cool place and back. But there's hope. Another season started around the last of August up north, as shadows began to fall across the Pole and Arctic coolness edged south. It's about time to open caribou season in the Northwest Territories, and moose season in Newfoundland. As all those big orange buses start carrying youth to schoolhouses that are no longer little or red, the northern big game season gets underway, and the Carolinas are still trying to beat the heat.

Then, out of deference to a long, hot and alternately too wet or too dry summer, officialdom opens dove season, just to keep the natives quiet. Aside from outlawing football, failure to open dove season would be most likely to cause a revolution here. The sight of those boxes of shells, the feel and heft of the old double-barrel, the hopeful look in the dog's eyes as it watches the wiping down of polished steel and smooth walnut are enough to stir the spirit. Then comes the first faint whiff of wood smoke, and one remembers the crunch of dry leaves and the pungence of burned gunpowder.

Yessir, good times are a-coming. As soon as the welcome coolness of longer nights lowers the temperature of rivers and ponds the fish will again consider cooperating. As great flocks of birds gather to ponder flight plans for the southern migration, up north the ducks and geese are stirring, the immature testing their flight powers. Somewhere the sumac is making a turn to scarlet. Squirrels are working over hickory and oak and poaching pecans. As nights grow longer and cooler, the stars seem nearer. It won't be long before the trout come to life again and other fishes congregate in the sounds for a seaward migration. Great blankets of early morning fog fill lowlands and valleys. Buck deer, antlers still in velvet, stomp nervously, for the rut is not far off. The mast has reached its maximum.

In the high country, elk are beginning to bugle. The big bulls, leaving their bachelor ways to collect harems, are testing their strength against lodgepole and ponderosa for the forthcoming battles to be fought in forest glades. To the victor belongs the harem, but only for this season. Along the coast, flounder are waiting in the sounds and will soon attract the surf fisherman. Already the first big spot runs have begun off the ocean piers, and the jumping mullet are filling the nets of fishermen in the sounds. The harvest moon is growing, and the hunter's moon will soon follow. Football and doves, fishing and camping. If only one can survive the summer. It's autumn that will make it all worth while. Good times are a-coming.

MULLET BLOW

Mullet blows occur from the "false" blows of late August and early September to the "true" blows of mid-September into October.

The late summer sun still lies heavy on the land, and it has been too hot to fish. Besides, they aren't biting. So I've been sulking in the shade of *Sylvia II*. Well, maybe not exactly sulking, nor in the shade. I've been applying bottom paint. Bottom paint, for the uninitiated, is something routinely applied at least every six months to the underwater parts of boats. In referring to boats, I do not mean those buzz-things that ride around on trailers or are taken off shelves by fork lifts every weekend to drag people on skis or to drag bait and lures in front of fish that aren't biting. I am talking about boats that reside perpetually in salt water. Like houses, they need spring and fall cleanings, and then some.

Now about this paint part: it is a mixture of dissolved copper, creosote, tar, kerosene, and other valuables. Yes, I did say valuables. Have you priced a bucket of dissolved pennies lately? Nor have I, but the stuff I'm putting on the boat would, per gallon, destroy most of a C-note. This, by the way, is the cheap stuff, fisherman's red. The high-priced substitute can be had in quart size for the same denomination. This may explain why it is applied with such care and tenderness. Besides being too expensive to allow it to drip, it's the only thing that will practically repel bugs, worms, barnacles, sow duds, oysters, sawfish, filefish, oyster drills, and bottom drills, plus a host of other varmints that prefer the bottom of a boat to almost anything.

To paint a boat, you must get under it, really under it, to view it from beneath amidst sand, shells and sawdust, in order to stroke it, from stem to stern, with utmost care, affection, and, especially, a brush full of paint. If an upstater ever notices the healthy, ruddy glow of a typical boatman, it isn't just from sun and wind. It is mainly red bottom paint. When you haul a boat, certain weather conditions prevail: sun beating down so blistering that the paint boils, or rain in torrents, or both. And good help is hard to get, so you can't say too much when someone cleans a paint brush across your back, especially if it's your wife. Doubt that I'll get barnacles there.

I am confident that when *Sylvia II* is launched this time I will be truly king of the sound, ready for fall and winter cruising, with all troubles forgotten except for the bill. I'm even making plans for a sort of triumphal cruise, although I also said that before Memorial Day, Flag Day, Mecklenburg Independence Day, the Fourth of July, and Bastille Day. Come the first bona fide mullet blow—and I'll be judge of what's bona fide—*Sylvia II* will be queen of the waterfront.

∽∽∽∽∽∽∽∽∽∽∽∽

We're in that magic time of transition when the sun is returning ever closer to the equator and setting noticeably earlier each evening. As the nights grow steadily longer, the evening stars are clearer, for the late summer haze, red and sweaty, is giving way to the cooler, drier air that is breaking free from the far north. Already the leaves are thinning, worn and limp from the heat and glare and whipping sou'westers. Their grip on life is loosening. Soon they will be drifting to earth to provide a mulch, a blanket, to return the nutrients for reuse by new, oncoming life. The harvest moon gains strength, heavy dews wet the grass with sparkling sequins, and thoughts begin to return to blankets and possibly a jacket in the evening. The tempo of cricket song is slowing. Frogs and peepers barumph and peep a little less loudly.

At this season we make short cruises that will let us fish a little, watch the sun set and the stars come out, then make a brief run home after dark. On one such cruise we found a little slough between two shoals just off the main channel. I stood on the foredeck watching the anchor line pay out. *Sylvia II* drifted with the current until the flukes dug in sharply. I let out a few more yards, then secured the line to the Samson post. For several moments I stood there trying to take it all in: the orange-rimmed clouds to the west lying low over the water, and white shafts of light playing overhead; grassy little islands, awash at high tide, appearing as dark imperfections on the calm waters; tall, angular blue herons standing motionless, watchfully poised in the shallows; a trio of terns wheeling by in formation. I joined Mary and the others in the cockpit to watch the waters in the last of the fading light.

A riffle disturbed the water: a spray of minnows and a large Spanish mackerel leaping clear of the surface in hungry pursuit. A gull swooped in to hover above the action, anticipating a late snack. The pewter glint of the water marked last-minute feeding frenzies, and a final calm returned. The tide was changing now, and *Sylvia II* was swinging uncertainly. The blue-white moon reflected from an apparently motionless sound, but the tug of the ebb was beginning to pull at the anchor and the water gurgled lightly around the bow. Along the mainland shores, lights of homes glistened like strings of yellow and green beads.

When one is a dreamer, one sometimes sees certain things in a different light. I wondered how the scientific mind, like the mathematician's, looks at stars. Does it see them only as degrees and angles to form an astronomical calculation? Just about midnight the constellation Pleiades rises from the eastern horizon, and the Big Dipper is sinking into the northern woods. Before dawn Orion appears, marked by the hunter's distinctive belt. The Indian saw the Belt as that time when the frost begins to cover the land, observing that as long as Orion is visible there will be cold.

A fisherman might see Pisces, now overhead, as the sign of the fish. After all, this is the time of the best fishing. Yet some mystic sees it as a time when a dark stranger enters your life to relieve you of money—though that may be closer to April 15. The month past was the time of the spider, appropriately, for more spiders have been swinging by on invisible cables and spreading their webs across corners of porches than at any other time of the year. October is the month of yellow leaves. The dreamer? He can make it all fit. The man of scientific bent can give answers, too. While I'm not about to knock the mathematics route—I've never tried it—I do think dreaming is more fun.

We lay at anchor until the moon had neared the horizon, then reluctantly started the engine and upped anchor. The probing spotlight found the reflector of the day beacon that marked the entrance to the creek. Dark shadows contrasted with wavering reflections. We slipped in quietly, circled the little bay, and slid to the dock.

At this time of year the cold dry winds that whip away summer heat spread their cooling touch across the warm, suffocating ponds in white-capped ripples, stirring the heat-drugged fish in revival. Here on the coastal plain the first shiver runs through the sounds, and as the chill penetrates, sucking off the heat, the shallow water life forms stir and seek warmer water. Frogs, salamanders, and turtles sink a little deeper in the comforting muck. New sensations cause the mullet and trout to gather in deeper water and wander closer to the main channels, where the fall rains have washed in sweetness to mingle with the brine.

Ashore, where the gray skies meet the swaying marsh grass, the fishermen, too, feel the changes. Birds respond and start donning their fall and winter plumage. The raccoon's fur thickens, and the opossum hurries from meal to meal a little faster. Soon deer will enter the rut, and on the beaches the mullet fishermen will be seen sitting atop high dunes watching for schools of fish, their long seines neatly folded, ready to be paid out from surf boats.

∽∽∽∽∽∽∽∽∽∽∽∽∽∽∽

There is a fine art to the pursuit of the elusive clam. Almost any-one can stumble over a clam shell, but it takes one of us hard-core clammers to get a basketful. I now speak with great authority, having had my beginner's permit renewed. When Randy Willis, fisherman and philosopher, asked us to go clamming, it had seemed a good idea, and we could find no unreasonable excuse for refusing. We were to meet at two, to catch the last of the ebb. "Bring your own rake," Randy added. There were but two rakes and one anchor in the hard-ware store. My pea digger was pre-occupied. Besides, I'd always wanted a genuine, factory-made clam rake like all the tourists have. In selecting clam rakes, look for the hook in the teeth, the spring of the steel. Each tine should be narrow and sharp, according to my clam digger's manual. The manual does not say what to do if the dealer has only one model and the boat is waiting.

Randy and his shaggy dog Salty were sitting patiently on the dock. Randy taped a patch over the oil cooler, cutting the water spray con-siderably. We cast off to head up the sound. Leaving the Waterway, we skimmed past the unmarked shoals, dodged fish stakes, rounded islands of waving marsh grass, twisting and turning through a laby-rinth of obscure channels. As I wondered at his uncanny sense of navigation, Randy laughed, "You are a white water sailor. I'm a yel-low water sailor." There is a world of difference. These waters change almost hourly. You've got to watch slicks and boils and wave pat-terns, besides having a sixth sense for understanding.

An immature gull watched us as we swung past a stake, brushed a large green marsh, eased around a point. Randy throttled back, shut down the engine, and dropped an anchor off the stern. "Skiff and wading from here in." The skiff he had in tow was a work- and weather-worn wooden boat, stable as a rock. Shiny plastic boats are for play-fishing. To get the feel of serious fishing, one should become intimately acquainted with rust-streaked hulls, battered and splintered rails and trawl boards, worn pulleys, the smell of diesel and stagnant bilge waters, salt- and scale-encrusted gear.

Clams come in various sizes and even a few different shapes. At first, I'd been confused about cherrystones and quahogs, littlenecks and steamers, gooeyducks and hardshells. After twenty-some years, I've got them almost straight. Quahog is the original name for the common hardshell clam we know here. It comes in big (chowder), small (cherrystone) and smaller (littleneck) sizes. Steamers and soft-shells are one and the same, but a Yankee species. Their undersized Southern kin are known as razor clams. Our hardshell clam is scientifically labeled *Venus mercenaria*, which makes sense, for a commercial clammer sure has to be mercenary.

There are three distinct clamming methods. There is kicking, by use of a boat propeller, which used to be considered illegal, immoral, and decadent, besides covering up and killing as many clams as it uncovers. Method Two is raking, which is the accepted, honorable way. Rake until a tine says, "Clunk." "Clinks" and "clacks" are scallop or oyster notes.

The third method is the least utilized and the most daring, but it's productive. It's called treading; I call it toeing. By either name, it is a warm weather procedure: dig in the mud and feel with the toes. Among the occupational hazards of toeing are great, mean toadfish that just love to clamp onto toes. There is a remote possibility of a man-eating clam grabbing you by the toe and holding you down as the tide rises ("remote" here refers to the South Pacific). And don't forget electric star-gazers, funny looking fish with high-voltage faces. Of all possible hazards, the worst and most likely is a broken beer bottle or a soft drink can well rusted on the edges.

As I said, toeing is productive. I remember Johnny Wetherington in his boatyard one time dropping a prop shaft nut in the mud. He toed five pecks of clams before he found the nut. It's a delight to watch the facial expressions of a toer. First, a sublime, blank stare into the heavens. Then a smile crosses the face and up comes a foot holding a clam between the toes. I'm told that a real toer can dig clams two at a time. There are no statistics on toeless toers, but I suspect that insurance companies would consider it a high-risk occupation. Randy doesn't use the toe method. He prefers the rake, claims he has got up to ten bushels in four hours with an inexperienced helper. Mary's being our helper didn't even bring us up to one bushel an hour. But we had enough for more than one chowder party.

The tide was flooding strong now. The sun bobbed red on the horizon, to disappear behind gold and gray clouds; a flight of pelicans made their way east; high above them gulls streamed towards their night's rest; black-backed skimmers, harsh voiced, wheeled and flashed white breasts to the orange twilight, cutting a shallow furrow in the backwaters with their orange-red bills. The current tugged at us as we passed flashy sailboats, outbound shrimpers, buoys leaning before the strong tide. It was past quitting time at the boat yard, and neat rows of charter sportsfishing boats were stabled for the night. Randy swung about and I cast a line to the dock. Above us, curious, pink-faced tourists peered out the windows of an air-conditioned restaurant.

∞∞∞∞∞∞∞∞∞∞∞∞

Fishing was better in the old days. Everyone knows that. A professor type tried to tell me that it wasn't necessarily so, that really we just remember the good days and catches and seldom the days we were skunked. But things were better. Fish were bigger, too. I've got witnesses.

Sitting in a porch swing and talking with Cap'n Darcy Willis, we found the conversation turning to fishing, as it usually does, and we got the story from him. Seems it was a quiet day at the Cape (Lookout) a good while back. The date is unclear, but the time is definite: the jetty was being built. The men were working from a big barge when some of the young blades got to talking about the old-timers' telling of the whaling fun they used to have.

Well, about this time a real whale showed up in the bight, so the fellows borrowed an "iron," jumped in the skiff, and took out after it. After a while they got close and let fly with the iron, just to show the rest how it was done. They had stuck it well, and the whale took off. But it headed the wrong direction, straight for shore. They hung on. In its leaping the whale discovered its error, made a somersault to reverse course, and took a heading to seaward. Cap'n Darcy claimed a ten-foot wall of water washed ashore, with them in the middle of it.

The reversed course was like playing crack-the-whip. Next thing the whalers knew, the animal was bound for the new jetty. Bouncing off the jetty, the whale charged around between rocks and barge and was last seen on a course for open sea. The survivors regrouped and made their way back to shore, satisfied. "'Twasn't the right kind of whale anyway," concluded Cap'n Darcy. It is known to this day as the Cape Lookout sleigh ride, demonstrating that not only were the fish bigger, but the big ones got away then, too.

※※※※※※※※※※※

By the time they reach Carolina, the first outbreaks of Arctic air are mere wind shifts that scarcely crack the heat of summer. Along the coast, the land and the people, still steaming in the hot humid weather that originated in Caribbean and Gulf, await what is known as a mullet blow. At first there are but a few false wind shifts; sooner or later the big shift will come. It will start perhaps with a ring around the moon, then a few high, thin cirrus clouds, lacy crystals of ice far up in the stratosphere that scarcely break the sun's rays. Inland, the change becomes apparent as winds freshen and large blue-black clouds rise above the western horizon, white capped, while turbulent winds and rain assault the earth. At last, cold Arctic air sweeps under moist tropical air, lifting it aloft to squeeze out the heat and moisture.

A mullet blow comes in varying intensities, but the real one is when the air behind is cold and dry, a whistling wind that switches to nor'west and bends trees, whitens wave tops, sends leaves swirling, and brings a sudden chill through overheated ponds, rivers, and estuaries. All summer the new crop of fish has been feeding and growing fat on the abundant food supply in the warm shallows of river and creek, but with the abrupt chill a primeval signal excites the mullet and its kin. Schools now leave the warm, thin waters and begin to gather in deep pools and channels.

The cooler waters, carrying new flavors from a storm-washed land, settle through the estuaries. Stimulated by new hungers and strange sensations, the fish begin to move. The migration gets underway slowly, each intensified cold front, each succeeding mullet blow stirring them into frenzied haste towards the inlets and the bitter brine of ocean. Schools of mullet move along the beaches as the September moon, which we know as the Harvest Moon, signals the regeneration of coastal fishing.

There is a certain social stratum that comes to life with the first movement of fish. Some writers sing of blue and white marlin; others of trout and mackerel, of flounder and drum. But by far the most popular sports fish on the coast is the spot, called at this season the yellowfin spot, seldom getting to a pound in weight. Not even known for its terrific fighting ability or any other spectacular quality, it is still undisputed leader in abundance and edibility.

I recall one fine autumn afternoon when Mary and I felt the urge to see what was doing on the ocean side. We wandered into a tackle shop there. Pausing at the counter with the usual "How's fishin'?" we got this enthusiastic answer: "Great! Really catching 'em!" Now we know pier operators: like other pros, they tend to exaggerate a bit. Down that long-legged extension of wood, nails, and bolts that jutted seaward, we could see maybe eight or ten bodies leaning listlessly against the rail. I had him cold!

"How come no fishermen?" Ken Bradley sighed, "Come here," and he flung open the door of a walk-in refrigerator to point out coolers, buckets, and boxes full of spots. Then he led me to the cleaning stand, where several anglers were dressing fish and putting them in big coolers. A fish scaler, like a giant clothes dryer, was buzzing away. "Come back tonight for the action," Ken suggested.

We returned two or three hours after sunset. The surf eased ashore lazily. The wind was light out of the north, with just enough chill to make a jacket welcome. The parking lot was filling up. Fishermen were converging on a pier already lined with anglers. They toted rods, tackle boxes, buckets, coolers. To watch spot fishermen congregate is like seeing a big orchestra assemble. The individuals gather, take their positions and wait, some passively. Others busily prepare large quantities of bait. Almost all station themselves on one side of the pier.

Some say it's part of the Great Fisherman's plan for spots to run at night. Else how would the working man be able to gather his winter supply? At first only an occasional fish was being landed, but the tempo was increasing slowly. There were steady flashes of fish and rods against the black sky, until two at a time was the rule.

The lights of town blinked like faraway fireflies. To seaward, the flashing red and green of inlet buoys kept a rhythm with the white sweeping flash of the distant Cape Lookout Light. Running lights of a ship showed intermittently between swells. As the pulse of fishing quickened, jugs of coffee were forgotten for more important matters like making the long hike to the tackle shop for more bait. The fish were coming over the rail like a shower. Idle talk had died down—this was serious fishing. And the boxes, buckets, and coolers filled up. It's not uncommon for a family to pick up two to five hundred spots in a night or two. It means that the day is devoted to cleaning, packing, and storing the night's catch. Spot runs may be intermittent, but often the fish run for all but a few daylight hours. Fever for spots is high among small boat anglers, too, when every weekend sees launching ramps crowded and everything that will float found inshore of the inlets along the Carolina coast.

A golden crescent moon was rising as we left the beach. Its slightly rippled reflection seemed to beckon us to follow. Behind us the fishermen kept baiting and casting and catching while the towns slept. Nighttime now belongs to the spot fisherman.

~~~~~~~~~~~~~~~~~~~~~~~~

Somehow, in the rush to participate in the better things of life, I failed this year to give proper recognition to the autumnal equinox, that magic time when nature signals that the summer curtain has fallen. Now the spirits of darkness are on the ascent, and shall rule. The earth in its wobble has tilted enough that the sun no longer passes north of the equator. In the land of aurora borealis the sun barely skims the horizon before dropping, until, in a month or so, the long night that will last from November through January will keep the snow and ice in continual darkness, broken only by the Northern Lights, the stars, and a cold blue moon.

In the Carolinas, crickets are chirping and the cicada is singing its final song of summer. Land birds are congregating for travel, and in the sounds and rivers fish keep on moving. Beaches are becoming lonely and storm-swept. Days are hot, nights are cool. The red of sumac, the winey hues of vines brighten the woods, and the sweet gum has taken patches of bronze. The Hunter's Moon is growing, and up around Hudson's Bay great rafts of Canada geese are gathering strength, feeding on grasses and wild rice shoals until northerly winds, any day now, will force the waters into the bay and flood the food supply. Sensing the oncoming severity of winter, they will assemble their family units to fly south through ice and sleet, passing high over farm and field and forest, undaunted. Below, the landsman will hear the lonely bark and step out into frosty air to listen to his free brother in the sky, escaping. He will wonder, and a little of him will go along.

The first snows have already hit the high country. Elk, nervously avoiding the two-legged stalkers that invade their domain, are sticking close to the dense shadows of the lodgepole slopes. Black bears are sitting in the huckleberry patches, scooping in purple mouthfuls of frostnipped berries that have turned to wine. Soon they will stagger off in a drunken stupor, to doze away the intoxication, and repeat the routine until the berries are gone or covered with snow.

〰〰〰〰〰〰〰〰〰〰

It was the last of September before *Sylvia II* made her formal and triumphal return to the downtown waterfront, the climax of months of restoration. The occasion was Heritage Week, the annual old boat reunion, which Mary calls the wooden-boat-weekend. The Chrysler

Crown engine, as old as the boat, never missed a beat as we headed for the festivities. We broke out the signal flags, unused for several years, and dressed ship. We had properly hoisted the Stars and Stripes before getting underway, and *Sylvia II* fairly strutted as she went down the waterfront. The sponsoring Mariners Museum committee hung a sign on her designating her as flagship and committee boat. Secretly, we figured it was because she was the only boat with signal flags. She looked mighty pretty that day, the last brushfuls of paint being applied to her new wood as she headed down to take her place in the middle of activities, flags fluttering in the sou'west breeze. I didn't tell anyone, nor was there a soul who knew what the signal flags spelled. "Sonny" Geer, waterfront oil dealer, had given us, years before when we were promoting sportsfishing, a set of flags that I'd carefully deciphered: "New Gulf Pride Marine HD Oil." No one had been the wiser.

As the tourists began to arrive I'd sought out Cap'n Theodore, sunning on his favorite waterfront bench, and invited him to bring the other retired captains to the boat. Among them was Cap'n Johnny Styron, skipper of the other *Sylvia*, that had berthed alongside our *Sylvia II*. Theodore took over and welcomed the guests. More than a hundred old customers, friends, acquaintances, and strangers signed the log that day, including the granddaughter of William Riley, Sylvia Willis Dillon, for whom the boat was named. She came aboard to be photographed for the *Carteret County News-Times*.

On the second day the races began. Cap'n Theodore, who'd skippered her for thirty-odd years, was duly piped aboard, and *Sylvia II* escorted the wooden sailboats on their race around Sugarloaf Island. All flags flying, she accompanied the last racer to the dock, and those long months of labor faded into memory. But the nostalgic weekend was not over: as we cruised contentedly back towards the creek, we were hailed by a great tug pushing two barges. We pulled alongside and exchanged courtesies with an old boating friend who had recognized us from afar. It was like titan and mosquito cruising together. The titan was *Patricia*, a Willis Barge Lines tug. The water world is close-knit, and even the women for whom the two boats are named are kin. Our friend Tom Kellum was first mate of *Patricia*, and he clocked *Sylvia II* at eight knots, a fair turn of speed for a lady who'd been through so much.

I remember that the first tow we ever passed with *Silver Spray* on her maiden voyage to Florida was *Chauncey*, of the same Willis Barge Lines. The Intracoastal Waterway is a kind of interstate for commercial and pleasure craft. It was developed for "providing a protected passage inside, safe from storms, shoals and perils of the sea." It offered excellent protection against the torpedoings common, though virtually unknown to the general public, during the last war.

A constant flow of barge traffic carries various cargoes, including grain and oil, and any small boat will frequently be meeting and passing these leviathans of the Waterway. While tugboats may be thought of as unattractive, even ugly, to us they are proud, handsome, and utilitarian, and they do their jobs well. However, one doesn't fool with them: escorting tows of hundreds and thousands of tons of cargo, it is impossible for them to get out of your way or stop within less than a mile or so.

But they give a sort of continuity to the Waterway. You may pass them by day and then, tied up for the night, or anchored in some cove or creek or horseshoe bend, you begin to feel and hear the heavy throb of their engines and see their ever-probing searchlights cut through the blackness like incandescent swords as they push on, no matter the fog or storm, ice or darkness. They excite the imagination with their strength and dependability. They may be going only as far as Port Everglades, but they impart a sense of faraway places.

The thought of following Tom south crossed my mind, now that *Sylvia II* was properly refloated and ready for serious cruising. There was no reason we couldn't swing the bow south and trail in the wake of *Patricia*. No fancy yacht, but with a little common sense, she could take the big open sounds as well as any plastic floating palace. When Tom is southbound and shines that big spotlight on our house, it does seem as if he's saying, "Follow me!" I'd have to bring this up to Mary.

There is a phenomenon that occurs every autumn along the coast. It is dependent on two factors. All summer in the warm, rich estuaries and sounds the fish have been feeding and growing, preparing for the days referred to Down East as a mullet blow. This is a time of rejoicing, for the long wait is over. The mullet blow gets the mullet on the move and the fishermen go out to net them.

The wind had swung around from southwest to west that day. Low gray banks of mist were moving across the sound in silent gloom. Worn and battered leaves of summer were falling, swept by the wind in fluttering migration like hungry birds, blanketing the still-green grasses with bronzes and yellows. A raft of mallards rode the surge behind a clump of marsh grass that waved, half submerged, along the shore. The raucous laugh of feeding gulls was following a school of fish that roiled the surface of the gray-streaked waters. Then the weather cleared and the fish got on the move. High on a windswept dune on the Banks, amidst tawny sea oats and salt-carved scrub oak, stood the lookout. A fisherman, studying the ocean, saw the school of mullet lying offshore, just beyond the reach of the crew that waited on the beach below. In the congregation were a blue pickup, a tractor, a skiff piled high with silver-gray net, and a half-dozen or so men.

Beyond the mullet a flock of birds was wheeling and diving. Another school of fish; these were blues, big and hungry, but also too far offshore. The parties aboard sportsfishermen riding the horizon seemed not to see the big fish, or were too preoccupied with fall kings to bother. Dotting the beach were the surfcasters, in clusters and singly, some lounging against beach buggies that bristled with rods. Others had hiked through the dense tangle of protective forest that lay between road and surf, to climb down the eroding dunes and cast their lot into the rolling surf. The surf appeared first as a low swell, rising as the shoals tripped it into a white cascade that thundered ashore, then hissing away to recoup its strength for another try.

When the moon goes down to the west, it's high water on this beach; but it was still well up in the sky. The mullet, moving with the current, had been stopped by something we couldn't see. The school split and moved back, the big fish roiling the sand as the crew watched. The net was tethered to the shore, and the skiff was launched into the surf, but for a while neither crew nor fish moved. Farther offshore a big shark cruised slowly. Frightened fish glittered silver as they leaped clear of the water to escape. The surfcasters tended their rods, occasionally picking up a spot or a pompano. Jumping mullet rarely take a hook, and the school of blues had passed far beyond the outer surf line.

It wasn't until high tide that the current picked up and the mullet began to move. The lookout signaled the waiting crew. The big skiff headed offshore, paying out the net astern. Then, swinging east, it paralleled the beach as the mass of fish moved towards its trap. They were nearly surrounded when the boat began to swing ashore. The fish sensed the net and broke in a massive attempt to escape. Some retreated, others sounded and still others leaped in confusion as the net closed, encircling them. Gulls that had been standing idly on the beach responded to the drama and rose screaming to reap the rewards. The net, both ends now ashore, was hauled in by hand and by tractor. Some leaped clear in frantic fright, but most were only confused.

The men, chest deep in the surf, stood on the bottom line of the net to keep the fish from escaping beneath until the great mass of quivering, flapping fish, aided by the force of the sea, was pulled ashore. The blue pickup was loaded with well over a ton of sand-encrusted, silver-sided mullet, and it took the assistance of the tractor to pull it free of the soft sand. The crew, natives of Carteret County, is one of the last beach crews in North Carolina. The tradition is dying, the contributing factors including low prices, lack of fish, poor markets, and other more profitable ways of making a living. The lookout is a Salterpath building contractor fifty weeks of the year and, like the others, drops everything when autumn's nor'easters become frequent. Then he goes mulleting, a heritage passed on from father to son.

There is a tendency to be ashamed of one's ancestry if one's forefathers labored, be it as fisherman, farmer, miner or woodsman. To many, the thought of working with hands and back means that the brain does not function. Yet the recreation of some of the world's greatest minds is fishing, farming, working with hands as well as brain. Although the practice of beach seining may fade from the scene, the trade of the fisherman is an honorable one, and should be a source of pride, always.

What comes next is the famed mullet roast, a welcome and celebrated event. Some fish are fried, some baked, and others stewed. A mullet, to be done justice, must be roasted. Early wood carvings and pictures show that this was a tradition long before white man trod these shores.

There are a few variations and improvisations, but to have the feast of your life it takes one or more good-sized jumping mullet, two to three pounds undressed, a cup of coleslaw, and six to a dozen hushpuppies per person, plus drinks as preferred. The Indian method is to gut the fish, insert a green stick (not pine) three to four feet long through the cavity and out the mouth. Do not bother to scale the fish, but salt it well, and when the salt has "struck through," that is, penetrated the flesh, rinse off the excess. Insert the stick deep into the sand at the edge of an open fire, rotating the fish occasionally until cooked through.

White man's way is to butterfly the unscaled fish, cutting it down the back rather than the belly. Remove the entrails and head, salt about an hour before cooking and roast Indian fashion, with this variation: nail the fish to a long board eight inches wide or more, and drive into the sand.

Today's method is a little fancier. Gut and remove the head of a fat, fourteen- to eighteen-inch mullet, butterfly it and salt heavily before putting it in the shade while you make the rest of the preparations. If you fear some varmint will steal the fish, put it in the refrigerator.

Fire up the charcoal grill, assemble butter or basting sauce, coleslaw, hushpuppies, miscellaneous condiments, and drinks. When the red-hot charcoal turns to gray, rinse the salt lightly from the fish, press dry with towels, and paint the flesh side with butter or sauce. Lay the fish on the grill flesh side down to seal the juices. Brown it lightly. Turn scale side down, roast slowly until cooked through, basting now and then.

Serve hot, in the now-charred skin and scales. You will discover why the Carolina mullet roast is the envy of the outside world. It is the climax of the year, the epitome of good living. You, too, will understand why fishermen consider a good jumping mullet worth waiting for.

INDIAN SUMMER

Indian summer is generally October into November, after the first frost. It starts warm, ends cool.

My wife had decreed that the new bunk boards for *Sylvia II* were passable and that we could spend nights on board. Personally, I like the pipe berths better, but I'm just the skipper. It was one of those days when a bit of morning chill hung on until a warm sun burned through the mists. The dew was still heavy when we fired up the antique Chrysler Flathead Six and cast off. Once out of the creek, we pointed the bow to the east'ard, gliding easily down the sound in company with John and Gretchen Wyatt, aboard their *Holiday*. Passing the waterfront, and the port where divers were crawling over the hull of an ill-fated vessel that had been snatched from the graveyard by courageous salvors, we felt mixed emotions. We admired the venturesome and exciting work they'd done to recover a ship that had lain several years on the bottom, and even wished them luck; yet did

132

not vessel and crew deserve to rest in peace? Often rapid destruction, by professionals and amateurs, of offshore wrecks seems like stripping a graveyard. Wrenching off portlights, binnacles, wheels, dynamiting hulks for scrap—are we vandals, harpies, when we do these things?

We cruised on through rivers, creeks, and cuts, into the Neuse, poking along, nosing into obscure streams, drinking in the late blooming and changing colors of marsh, swamp, and forest, dropping anchor here and there for exploration and loafing. Eastern Carolina holds a paradise of incomparable beauty and loneliness. A crabber tended his pots, and in the distance an occasional trawler passed. Like the birds and the beasts, they belong there, an integral part of the scene. In tiny villages contented people live in blissful isolation, enjoying a quality of life our leaders often can neither understand nor appreciate. Each group seems to pity the other.

We anchored in South River. The dog needed shore leave, so we dropped the Avon raft over the side, and all hands set off for shore. A beautiful sandy beach and the reds, golds, and mellowing greens of fall beckoned us. The bow hit the beach. The dog leaped joyfully ashore. The crew stood up and then—abruptly, frantically, launched again and dug the oars deep. It was just past mid-day, but howling hordes of native insects—mosquitoes—were on guard, protecting the tranquil beachhead. Swinging and swatting, we slowly defeated the army and they gradually retreated to lurk in the shadows. Except at sunset and sunrise, anchoring about a quarter-mile offshore proved safe. At sundown we, too, retreated, to the safety offered by repellent, screens, and spray.

<hr>

Have you ever been hit by a wild goose feather? Here's the way it happens: you're minding your own business when out of the sky comes a feather, floating, spiraling, drifting back and forth in the still air until, quietly, it hits you. Only then do you hear the far-off barking of geese. But now you are a marked person, somewhat as in those movies where the king slapped the kneeling figure over the shoulder with his sword and said, "Rise up, Sir Knight!" Well, a goose feather is a bit like that, except much better, because a knight is expected to run around rescuing damsels and all that. Today, in light of traffic, women's lib, and such, knightly business could be dangerous. Besides, the law doesn't expect men to behave in knightly fashion, might think you a weirdo and commit you to the loony bin; but more of that later.

On the other hand, if you happen to be one of those chosen by the goose feather, there's almost no end to the benefits. You can wander around in blissful abandon, smelling flowers, fishing, mucking about in woods and swamps, regarding the world from a hilltop, or counting daisies, and hardly anyone will think a thing about it. Oh, a few might describe circles in the air with a forefinger; others will shrug their shoulders and say you just can't help it; and a few busybodies may offer condolences to wife, girl friend, or family. But generally they will ignore you.

Soon you'll find all sorts of good things happening to you. First, once goosed by the feather you will quit worrying. Who cares if the boys in the hallowed halls of government are playing games? That's their problem. You can only feel sorry for them. The rent is due. The landlord is the one with problems. You can but sympathize, invite him in for a spot of tea and a discussion of Thoreau. You might even reform him. Shortly after one fellow we know was struck atop the head by the goose feather, he actually quit working in a factory and moved to the coast to live in a simple shack by the water. Dabbling his toes in the sound in summer, he accepted money and other bribes from tourists for letting them do the same.

There are many versions of this theory, but one of the more significant aspects is to be struck properly by the right feather. Now it is well known that the Indians of the Great Plains, with whom I was intimately acquainted as a child, had this feather bit down pat. It should be noted that some Indians spent so much time outdoors that their heads fairly bristled with feathers. Furthermore, eagles were flying overhead in those days more often than not, and anyone knows that eagles tend to be more warlike. This can be confirmed readily by pictures of, say, Sitting Bull.

Here in the South there is a rather common bird, the mockingbird, that sits around courthouses particularly, shedding feathers. These birds have very little influence, being rather lethargic. But on the coast natives claim that one winter day there were literally thousands of loons flying over. They're not sure what caused the birds to start moulting—some say it was purely natural—but since that time hundreds, even thousands, of coastal Carolinians have been unduly influenced by loon feathers. And just to keep the record straight, a loony bin is not a coastal Carolina pot in which loons are cooked. A loony bin is something else entirely. It is to be found inland and is filled mostly with folks unfortunate enough never to have been hit by a falling wild goose feather.

But there is a candidate for the falling goose feather. He came whipping into the creek in one of those very expensive plastic and chrome boats—the man with the golden eyes—while I was perched on a raft sanding the round stern of *Sylvia II* and Mary was doing a balancing act with a can of paint. She waved at him to slow down, and moments later a voice up the creek that had earlier been explaining the necessity of stout mooring lines and strong cleats shouted, "There goes one of those (censored) I've been talking about! Slow down!" As his wake turned boats on end the operator growled back, "The engines won't turn any slower!" In somewhat of a huff, he snorted the boat about and, with much engine racing, started out of the creek. Trying to be nice, I asked if he needed something. "Looking for gas," he answered. That day the gas salesmen were all out on their own boats, so I directed him down the Waterway, where he'd find gas and dockage within a mile. As he disappeared noisily from the creek, we noted his hailing port, Boston.

It was maybe an hour later on the waterfront over coffee that we noticed the same boat tied at the Gulf dock. Then this tall, distinguished-looking chap with deep, deep tan, wearing a necklace and all that modern stuff, strolled into the restaurant. I nodded, "Thought you were heading south. See you went the other way."

He collapsed onto a chair. "I am, but there's only 2½ feet of water in that (censored) sound, and the people in your creek aren't very friendly. I wouldn't spend any money there." It was only then that I noticed the color of his eyes. They were gold! I'd never seen golden eyes in a human.

He continued, "Fourteen days alone and I haven't seen a good-looking woman." He was ogling the waitress, whom I thought pretty nice-looking. In fact, the room was full of them. Perhaps he meant something else. All the while he was fingering a gold chain around his wrist, heavy enough to sink him if ever he fell overboard. And rings! I've seen diamonds, but these were like baseballs in massive gold mountings, on each pinky. "Can't find anyone to cruise with me. Talk about troubles! I've had 'em up to here. Tore the bottom out of the boat, cost me five thousand in repairs. Busted the props twice since then. My lawyer is suing the insurance company."

He lit another cigarette. "You see, I was executive vice-president of"—he named one of the country's largest publishing houses—"but my heart's gone bad." Other gems between drags were equally fascinating, like his boat having burned 137 gallons between Belhaven and Morehead City, a short run. The waitress stood with pencil poised. "What! No cod or scrod?" (It turned out there was no haddock either.) "What kind of place is this?" Sweetly patient, the waitress suggested clams or shrimp.

Now eating your words is not nearly so easy as eating clams, shrimp, or even cod, and next day we saw the Bostonian back in the creek, with an overheating engine. The people in our creek were going to get some of his money, after all.

~~~~~~~~~~~~~~~~~~~~

Somewhere on every waterfront is a gathering place where the watermen congregate. Sometimes it's a fish house or a bench in the shade of a tree, but usually it's a small café where coffee is dispensed. At some dreary hour long before the dawn, the faintly illuminated boats lie rocking easily in their stalls. A neon sign glimmers down the dew-wet street, and only a few parked cars are in sight. Two men appear from the shadows, open the café door, spilling the yellow light into the darkness. An old pickup grinds along the street, brake lights flaring as it pauses beside the building.

Inside, the aroma of fresh coffee brewing and a mingling of odors of bacon and burnt toast are wafted from the back where a hearty, white-clad cook sweats over a grill. At the bar a whiskery fisherman swigs hot coffee while a younger man tells a tall story to the waitress, a pleasant woman of middle years who has heard the jokes a thousand times before. The door bursts open and two men tramp in, exchanging greetings. Gradually the room fills, the bar first, then the tables in the rear.

There is the roar of a boat engine as it sputters to life. Skippers talk of their day's plans. Charterboat passengers, quiet and subdued, hover over steamy platters of eggs with hot biscuits or pancakes and smouldering coffee. Unused to pre-dawn hours, they peer down the channel towards blinking buoys, as if hoping for some trace of daybreak. By now the first of the boats are easing out of their slips, red and green running lights reflecting off the black waters. Late arrivals gulp grits and ham, hoping the boat won't leave without them. The skipper races the engines impatiently. Franc White and I were those late arrivals.

A slight swell from the southeast met us as we crossed the bar. The sun was rising clear and bright amidst a fantasy of clouds. A low band of dark clouds lay along the eastern horizon, their tops tipped with gold; overall an unbelievable arch of blue, green, and pink. To the west'ard the rest of the world was still in darkness. Franc and I stood on the deck of *Ebb Tide* as she skimmed across a peaceful sea.

"Looks like a nice day."

"Yep. Guess we lucked out on this one. Oughta be right good fishin'."

We had been scheduled to go the previous day but had arrived late, just as the boat had cleared the dock, leaving us standing on an abandoned waterfront, cameras in hand.

Autumn king mackerel fishing along the Carolina coast is the stuff of which true fish stories are made. The fish are big, in great abundance, and possess terrific fighting ability. Added up, it's a sports-man's dream. There is only one slight problem: weather is unpre-dictable. About an hour and a half after crossing the bar we observed the swells increasing noticeably. Occasionally Skipper Bill Williams would throttle back abruptly as we met an unusually large sea. That left us hanging in mid-air. Then it was a drop down the express ele-vator. Throttles open again, we'd speed on. The sun had faded under a slate-gray cloud layer. It might rain before evening. In the stern, Mate Johnny Day and the other passenger, Bert Hughes, a paraplegic in a wheel chair, prepared bait mullet, Johnny cutting thin strips from the sides, Bert feeding the remains to the hovering, screaming gulls astern.

The seas were getting rough now—we were perhaps twenty or thirty miles offshore—but *Ebb Tide* rode them well. A faint thought of possible seasickness passed through my mind as I clung to the ladder, trying to keep my legs under me. Franc looked a trifle green when he saw Johnny blissfully munching his breakfast, a big slice of pecan pie. An extra big sea, ready to break, towered over the bow. Bill slacked the throttles and eased over it neatly. Bert had wedged his wheelchair securely between a fishing chair and the ladder I was hanging onto. A black cloud hung low over the water. The wind had picked up and rain began slashing across the seas, sizzling like a hot poker. Bill secured the bridge and transferred to the deckhouse controls.

Another sportsfisherman, *Tripoli*, already at the fishing grounds, could be heard by radio between the hisses and blurps. The skipper was watching us. "Getting a bit rough, eh? Weather don't look too good." That was the understatement of the week. "Look, we're less than five minutes from the rock," and Bill looked up from his loran screen. "We've come this far. Let's give it a pass or two." Lines over-board. Bert took one of the aft chairs. Franc and I took our places. I was definitely out of tune. Somehow in all the bouncing, twisting, and rolling, my eyeballs seemed to have come uncaged. Franc looked truly white. I had never known him to be seasick. He clutched at the rail and leaned over. Bill turned the boat, putting the stern to the giant seas. My eyes wouldn't focus. Dizzy, I tried to reach for the rod and missed. Johnny thrust it into my hands.

A slamming yank nearly lifted me out of the chair. "Strike!" I heard faintly. I aimed at the rail, offering breakfast, dinner, lunch, and perhaps previous nourishment to the sea gods. I was still reeling when there was a pounding at the stern, the line went slack, and a voice announced a fish in the box. I didn't see it, but I felt wonderful relief, and my eyes began to slow down. Now Franc had a fish on. I grabbed his camera, pointed it in the general direction and pressed the button, hoping it, at least, was in focus. I tried to get off my knees, but every time I got one leg under me the boat would heave another direction, skidding me across the deck.

Bert seemed to be having the time of his life, reeling in a big one. I handed the camera to Franc as I slid by. It was his turn. Regaining the chair and my rod, I had another strike. This one I saw. It was the first time I ever pulled a fish down to me. It was on the crest of a looming wave when the wave literally fell out from under the fish. Then Franc had another fish on. Sick as a dog, he alternately reeled and heaved. Now he was interesting green and red hues. Johnny gaffed the fish. A sea hit again. This time I was unprepared, and the swivel chair swiveled. Round and round it went, the tossing of the boat adding momentum, until finally someone grabbed me and stopped the merry-go-round.

Time crawled by, each minute seeming like three hours. Then Johnny began hauling in the lines. Bill had swung the boat to the north'ard. "Let's put her in the barn, boys. She's gettin' too rough out here." Going with the seas was easier. I was feeling much better. Bert, never fazed by ricocheting in his wheelchair, joined me in the cabin. Johnny's work done, he crawled into a bunk. Franc still sat slumped over in his chair on the stern deck. A wall of rain deluged us. He looked pitiful, water running off him in torrents. His orange foul weather clothing glistened, the only bright spot in view. Obviously he was beyond caring.

The seas were ten to fifteen feet now, with a strong sou'west wind picking up rapidly. The ocean was a menacing deep olive-green, rolling by with white water riding the crests. The inlet was the roughest. By this time Bill and I had returned to the bridge. One huge sea sent *Ebb Tide* sliding downhill on her side, her bow slipping into the bottom of the chasm. Her roll was so extreme that I was convinced she'd laid over by the breaking sea following close astern. I was sure that my weight on the bridge would be the final straw.

Franc, who had been moved into the cabin for safekeeping, looked up and was sure we were about to capsize, but was too numb to care. He lay forward on the dinette table, head on his arms. I was looking at the ugly green waters directly below me, waiting, when *Ebb Tide* began to recover.

Once inside the jetty, we let Franc know he had survived. At dockside we gathered gear, took pictures of the catch, thanked Bill and Johnny, and headed home. I was hungry, having been relieved of several meals, and Franc had recovered. Actually, the trip had been great and the fishing good, but I was willing to give the big kings a rest until another year.

~~~~~~~~~~~~~~~~~~~~~

Upstate folks predict winters by the woolly bears, that larval form of the tiger moth. They measure the red band in the center vs. the black ends. The wider the red band, the more severe the winter. If one measures the right woolly bear, forecasting can be incredibly accurate. But down here on the coast I've discovered another, more reliable way of foreseeing the winter: measure pinfish. The bigger the pinfish, the colder the winter. It stands to reason, for if a bear or woodchuck fattens up to hibernate for a cold winter, then why shouldn't a fish? So far I haven't proved the theory, but this winter should tell the tale, because the biggest pinfish in recent history are being caught right now. Normally, a pinfish, the most common species caught off docks and seawalls, runs an average of four to six inches. But this fall claims of nearly a pound are common.

Like autumn colors in the mountains, the season brings a changing scene to the coast. Waterfronts are loaded with boats, mostly big city types heading south by power and sail. From hundred-foot palaces with chromeplated crews to rusty, leaky tubs propelled mainly by luck and inspiration, there's always a character boat or two. Now is the season for boat watching, a hobby that can border on being a profession. It gives hours of speculation and pleasure, and the waterfronts of Morehead City and Beaufort are the finest observation grounds anywhere on the coast. There are thirty to fifty boats, mostly sail, in Beaufort any given day. On the Morehead City waterfront a few sailers can be found in the anchorage that was once the turning basin for the big menhaden fleets that used to fish out of here every fall, but sleek yachts and sportsfishermen take up the rest of the available space. Trawlers festooned with nets and colorful chafing gear are always a part of the scene, as well as a longliner occasionally, with lines and hooks and gaudy floats carefully arrayed for the next trip to sea. "Boaters" have been replaced by the real watermen, the small crabbers and clammers who slip in and out almost unnoticed, and the charter fleet that still fishes inlet, shoals, and offshore. For the transients, fleeing the onset of winter, the adventures lie ahead. Nowhere are changing seasons more vividly dramatized than on the waterfront.

When the charter boats begin to unload the sportsfishing equipment and replace the fighting chairs with fish traps stacked high on deck, while others move up the creeks, and the waterfront begins to look deserted, then you know that Indian summer is over. Before the icy winds whip across the still-warm sea and the water begins to smoke, it's time to gather firewood. Frank Bayer had a big old hickory alongside his home. The tree was nearly dead, and the way it leaned over the house looked ominous for the roof. Immediately after it was cut we began reducing it to firewood, for a hickory gets increasingly hard while you're standing there debating where to cut first. Discovering that the chain saw wasn't working at all well, we got busy with the whip saw. A whip saw is so named because when you are through with it, you are thoroughly whipped.

While I regained my breath after just one cut, curiosity prompted us to try dating the tree. The outside ring marked the year officials were telling us not to eat sage hens from Montana because of pesticide poisoning, but the osprey and eagle count was up because of the banning of DDT. Meanwhile Congress was wrangling, trying to decide whether or not to allow mineral exploration in designated wilderness areas. By now we were slicing into 1972, the year that man made his last trip to the moon via Apollo Lines. In this same era of widening horizons, one pilot with tunnel vision, working for a Wyoming rancher, killed 570 eagles, though a few more cuts would reveal 1940, when it became unlawful to kill bald eagles. Even in the 1960s, when man was beginning his attempts to travel beyond the earth's atmosphere, a conservationist was still considered a bit addled.

More sweat now as the saw cut beyond the Korean War and into World War II—only forty-eight states then. Cutting was getting noticeably stiffer as the saw bit into the heartwood that was formed during the depression and the days of the CCC. Those were the years when the first modern wildlife management programs began. Somehow the tree had survived the great land speculation boom of the 1920s, when the real estate boys promised a cozy cottage in every swamp, and the Migratory Bird Act was signed into law in 1929. And then we had sawed beyond my time, when the last flights of geese and ducks were sweeping down from the northland, drastically reduced, and wildlife was at perhaps its lowest ebb. We cut into World War I, when Dad was courting Mother, and back into the earlier 1900s, when the Panama Canal was dug and the Department of Agriculture was first authorized to close seasons on migratory birds.

Now that I think of it, we'd sawed right through radio and television, as accustomed as we'd become to these devices. We had reached the time when there were few cars and no land-devouring interstate highways. I was still wiping off sweat, even though it was a cold day, just as we cut into the days of Teddy Roosevelt, the first conservationist president. It seemed the last-of-everything era: the last ivory-billed woodpecker, the last sharp-tailed grouse, the last passenger pigeon. But it was also near the last of the market hunter, a species deserving extinction.

My arms ached, I was sure my back was broken, and I wished that

Frank had got the chain saw fixed. We were almost to the center now: the Spanish-American War, the last great slaughter of the Indians (we had already come close to exterminating buffalo, elk, and antelope). But somewhere an Indian had managed to hide a half-dozen buffaloes that would be the basis for the future, and the old tree was to live to a time when the great beasts were again roaming the range. The saw reached the core of the old hickory about 1875. Granddad had just married Grandmother, and they were heading for Dakota Territory in a covered wagon while a squirrel was burying a hickory nut close by a Carolina creek. It had survived a century before being stacked high in my back yard, destined to keep the Franklin stove glowing through many a cold night.

WHEN THE WATER SMOKES

During the transition of autumn into winter, when warm sea water meets cold air, the result is steam. It may be in fog, but more likely windswept "smoke."

The waterfront will soon close down officially. The tourists are all gone now, and a few red-faced, blue-nosed fishermen can be found in the lee of the fish houses, soaking up the southbound sun while a bitter north wind whips the dust and litter of summer down almost deserted streets. By the end of November most restaurants will be closed, but not for lack of business. Now locals can eat without being jostled and crowded by upstaters. Resorts are like that—as with favorite kinfolk, they're glad to see tourists come, glad to see them go. Nor is it just because heating of barn-like structures over the water is a great expense. It's also that waitresses, cooks, and management feel the need of a rest. The waterfront gift shops stay open for the Christmas trade, but when there is no place for the fishermen to hang out, the enjoyment is gone.

The fishing? One recent winter charterboat skipper George Beds-worth proved that king mackerel are available almost all winter, if one is willing to buck the elements, the cold and the bad weather coming closer together. Winter seas, as any seaman will tell you, are heavier. A fifteen-knot summer wind is a zephyr, while in winter it's a half-gale that can become a slammer. And sportsfishing is supposed to be fun, even for the crew. Besides, now's the time to rest and recoup and spend one's hard-earned income, what's left of it. In a good year a charterboatman is on the go seven days a week, sixteen to eighteen hours a day. He hasn't time to go to the movies or ride around in the car for pleasure. He hasn't time to take his family on a picnic. So, along about the tail end of fall, winter gales offer a relief he can get no other way. We consider the sportsfishing season over when Cap'n Leroy Gould brings his *Mattie G II* back to Peltier Creek.

Thanksgiving in early America filled a similar need, and was stretched into a week or more of turkey and pumpkins, sweet pota-toes and ham and cranberries, all "as American as apple pie." Home folks still see it as a time when the men come back red-faced and bones aching from greeting the frosty morning in a duck blind away out in some remote marsh. A hot toddy and a snapping fireplace radiate cheer and warmth into the home. There is the smell of woodsmoke and roasting fowl, a turkey or a goose. In the West it's pheasant and the sweet, steaming pungence of spices. You can go walking in the woods, a blanket of leaves crunching underfoot while chickadees and warblers flit ahead through the brush and squirrels chatter high on the sprawling limbs of an oak. There is the crack of wood as an ax bites into the fibers and makes firewood, the shine of a frost-bitten lawn beneath the moon's cool light. Overhead the cluster of stars known as the Pleiades is in view, and Orion the Hunter rises strongly in the east.

Hunter or not, each of us can give thanks for the flights of water-fowl that dot the red skies of morning, for the rabbit, the grouse, and the woodcock exploding underfoot, for the good friends who share our attainable goals. Now is the time also to appreciate the

145

bountiful land of white-tail and dove, and a nation awakening to the value of its natural resources.

~~~~~~~~~~~~~~~~~~~~~~~~~~

Walking across the yard the other morning, I heard a dull boom from the house next door. I sprinted over to find Gary Burnham sitting on the floor, anxiously checking his beard. Two other fellows were looking in surprise from bedroom doorways. Then I noticed the stove. It was several inches from the wall. The top was ajar, and every door, drawer, tray, and movable part had moved. Then Paul Carlson was saying, "No, Gary, you light the match first, *before* you turn on the gas."

It seemed only natural to me, for Gary is a Mohawk Indian and I'd already learned that Indians often have a dramatic way of doing things. You see, a retired Boy Scout from Alabama, later drummed out of Dan Beard's legions, claimed that he and the Green Berets had been taught how to start a fire Indian-style, and he'd gone ahead to prove his point. Imagine lying peacefully in your sleeping bag beside a lake in the Canadian bush. Sunrise is being considered as the grayed embers of last night's fire emit a faint column of smoke, when up strolls our hero, announcing like Beelzebub that he's going to start the campfire. He tosses a Dixie cup of gasoline (unleaded) into the ashes. The resulting explosion scorches neighboring trees and burns a hole in the heavens. You can understand why since that time, on any trip with this old Scout, my wife is overeager to start the campfire. It has developed into a race between the two to see who will be keeper of the fires, and no longer do I risk laying my sleeping bag near the fire in the Scout's camp.

Generally one experiences a sense of well-being in the presence of a genuine outdoor type. Indoors, though, may be a different matter. Jim Dean had invited us over to his cottage on the beach one cool evening. We were sitting around enjoying delectable refreshments when he decreed that it was cool enough for a fire in the fireplace. As card-carrying fire watchers, we agreed. Oh, he had all the right stuff, no question: the proper tinder, kindling, and hardwoods. But soon I noted, being the tallest in the room, that something was interfering with vision and breathing. "Takes a while to warm up," Jim explained. I ducked under the pall of smoke to help fling open doors and windows. It made no difference. Next, braving the inferno, I checked the chimney for an obstruction. And there was one. Outdoor campfires do not have dampers. Indoor fireplaces do, and this one was closed tight.

Still, this sort of thing is not new. I know of one man who bought a house because he particularly liked the fireplace. He complained, though, that it wouldn't draw. It took somewhere between five and nine years before he discovered that the handle on the wall was for opening the damper. This is not to suggest that fireplaces and chimneys haven't been a problem to me, too. The chimney to our Franklin stove was a rude, crude affair that was neither safe nor secure, so I decided to put in a patented insulated pipe directly above the stove instead of having the pipe wander throughout the house before exiting. I summoned a local tin bender, and he arrived with gear. "Where do you want it?"

Well, let me tell you, it's darned hard to guess where the stove is from atop the roof, and I needed a straight line. Then it dawned on me: an easy way. I got the .22 out of a closet, plumbed it with a level, and sent Mary out to clear the roof area. She had to argue some with the tin bender to get him off the roof where he'd stationed himself to watch the bullet come through. When I got the all-clear signal I let fly. A .22 is noisy enough inside a house to be impressive, but it didn't penetrate the roof. I substituted a .22 magnum for the long rifle—now that *is* noisy—but still no hole. Perplexed, I dug out the old .30-30. That rattled every window, but would not penetrate a two by six on edge. We finally got a hole through the roof, but the pipe is just a tad out of plumb. While the tin bender thought it was the best solution to obtaining a vertical line he'd ever heard of, myself, I think there has to be a better way, for my ears are still ringing.

As you can see, fireworks have always played an integral role in our lives, although my wife admits that housecleaning isn't quite as exciting as when my oldest brother was here. In those days brother and I did a lot of shooting at targets and reloading ammunition. From time to time, Mary undertook to clean what she called the powder room. She's pretty savvy about firearms, but what she hadn't given a second thought to was the wastebasket at the end of the work bench. She picked it up and blithely emptied it into the incinerator, tossed in a lighted match and strolled back towards the house.

Next thing Mary knew there was this whoosh as a mushroom cloud ascended, then a series of bangety-bangs, like a Chinese New Year celebration. From her refuge behind a porch post she heard whoom! boom! blam! like an old Batman film, as holes began to appear in the side of the steel oil drum that is now our ventilated incinerator. What she didn't know was that Jim had spilled a can of black powder, which mingled with some smokeless, so he'd brushed it all into the wastebasket, along with a few spent primers and a handful of dead mercury batteries. She has avoided the powder room cleaning detail ever since.

That reminds me of Charlie McNeill's maid. She was cleaning the kids' closet. Everything went, including a big paper bag of junk which she deposited in the incinerator. She, too, applied a lighted match and had bent over to pick up something else, when the boys' sizeable inventory of fireworks started going off in all directions. As we understand it, Charlie still finds maids hard to come by.

⌇⌇⌇⌇⌇⌇⌇⌇⌇⌇⌇⌇⌇⌇⌇

With cold weather already upon us, I knew *Sylvia II* should be hauled and painted again soon, just in case. The difference between winter and summer down here is that the bad weather comes closer together in winter. By January we can count on a few hard freezes where the fresh water creeks will turn to ice for up to a week at a time, followed by intermittent rain and sunshine. I found myself thinking more and more about taking the boat south before too many more weather changes. My reasoning was valid: as an elderly but still spry lady, she might like the taste of Florida's warm sweet waters after all she'd been through. I knew that I would. I even mentioned it to Mary one morning—casually, you know. She didn't say yes; but she didn't say no, either. I eeled out of the house in order not to seem too eager.

Three pelicans, bellies reflecting red from the early morning sun, soared through the narrow creek entrance on silent wings as I stepped aboard the boat to meditate on the probable cost of repairing a leaky through-hull fitting. Replacing the threaded bronze fitting wasn't impossible, excessively expensive, or even difficult, but somewhat like grabbing a loose strand on a sweater and running—it can lead to a lot of things, most of them not so good. It has always seemed that, if one has enough patience, everything will come in time, or go away, yet a leaky fitting can be worrisome, at best. Not being ready for the boat to go away, I took a deep breath, started the engine and headed for the marine railway.

Modern "boaters"—those folks with plastic skimmers and trailers— are really missing something when they bypass boatyards. It was a slack time at Taylor's yard, though *Phalarope* was sitting high and dry, getting a facelift. Men scurried about, dealing in mahogany, teak, and fiberglass. On a table glittered an array of bronze port-lights. Cabinet makers and ship's carpenters fashioned wood into patterns of beauty and function, while a masked man sprayed mysterious materials that solve all boating problems.

Warren Taylor dispatched two men to an unoccupied railway, and soon the dripping, barnacle- and slime-covered bottom of *Sylvia II* emerged from the cold, dark creek into the harsh world of air and man. I feel little compassion for barnacles gasping for life-giving water. Rather, my attitude is, Serves you right for attaching to anything of such beauty, instead of to a piling. To replace a hull fitting can lead to a succession of adventures, scraping and sanding, testing seams and fastenings, inspecting for worms and fleas. Yes, boats can get fleas—some folks call them gribbles—that look like a cross between flea and shrimp, but *Sylvia II* was not so afflicted. You should also check for electrolysis, bad bearings, and anything else you can see or hear.

After due thumping and poking, I stepped back to contemplate while trying to wipe the grime from my hands. A figure appeared in the doorway of the boat shed. The soft voice of Mike Alford said, "Mind if I take her lines?" Now in some circles it might be considered insulting to ask to take a lady's lines, but Mike is, above all, a gentleman. He is also a naval architect who modestly refers to himself as "just a marine designer." As a historian, he spend his time searching out old boats and recording their shapes and designs for the archives of Hampton Mariners Museum in Beaufort.

Boat builders, old craftsmen of Carolina, "seldom ever" used a blueprint to build a boat. Many still don't, but never let it be said that they don't know what they are doing, for tucked away upstairs is more experience and practical knowledge than many of today's designers and builders can hope for. Today, with the age of cheap and theoretically unlimited energy coming to a halt, we are realizing that those old-timers did know what they were about. In the late 1970s two boats, one a forty-foot modern houseboat, the other a fifty-five-footer built along old lines, made a three-hundred-mile cruise together, both traveling at about the same speed. The boat of old design burned 222 fewer gallons of fuel.

The keel of *Sylvia II* was laid in the early 1930s, but her lines are much earlier. Low power and high efficiency were still important then. Recent efforts that have been made to emulate the old designs may, along with woodburning stoves, insulation, and the use of sun and wind, be a signal that American thrift and greater efficiency are reemerging in today's land of waste makers. Mike and an assistant stretched string, erected poles, dangled plumb bobs, measured angles and distances of rake, sheer, turn of the bilge, garboard, keel, stem, stern, and all that nautical jargon. Meanwhile I kept tripping over the strings. If the boat's lines turn out a little funny, it'll be my fault. Until rejected, *Sylvia II* is a national, or state, or surely a Peltier Creek, treasure. We'll submit her name to the Trust for Historic Maritime Preservation. A grant or two of public money may be forthcoming, and I can cruise in style. *Old Ironsides* may be nudged aside. In the meantime, I'll sit on my stern, mug of yaupon tea in hand, waiting for my ship to come in, and savoring Mike's final compliment, "Her bottom has just as nice lines as her topsides." Now I ask you, isn't that a fine thing to say of a great little lady?

~~~~~~~~~~~~~~~~~~~~~~~~~~~~~~

For a trial run after putting *Sylvia II* back in the water, we took some friends to Shackleford Banks, little more than an hour from the creek. There was no bather, no surfcaster to relieve the loneliness of the wind-wrapped dunes. A fresh wind, west-nor'west, whistled across the open sound, whipping up whitecaps as the retreating tide met the force of the gusts. Dry grasses rattled, and the breeze picked up the singing sands and flung the grains across the beach. A pair of terns was balancing on the updrafts. We wandered the strand, almost oblivious to the low rumble of the surf.

Beaches, lonesome beaches, are among the most fascinating places in the world, receivers of the flotsam and jetsam of many seas, a mysterious world apart, teeming with life to a large extent unseen. How can one forget the lure, the constant rediscovery? That black object yonder—is it a fish box, a broken piling, a hatch cover from a boat at the bottom of the sea, or perhaps something still living? Maybe a mop handle, a worm-eaten shell, a timber from a long-lost ship, a piece of deck cargo, or the abandoned carapace of a horseshoe crab? Close examination may reveal it to be a sand-blasted bottle or the exquisite beauty of a pen shell. Somehow all such useless items take on a romantic significance.

Behind the beach in the ghost forests, the shifting sands have uncovered twisted, silver-frosted skeletons of live oaks and cedars, buried in some forgotten time by ever-migrating dunes. Blowouts leave some of the deep hollows between dunes barren and wind-scoured, while others are pockets of closely cropped grasses, marsh pennywort, and scattered clumps of struggling cedar and yaupon, perhaps the site of a future maritime forest that will spring up, bloom, then be overtaken by the marching sands.

When we topped a dune to stand high above the landscape, we could observe both sound and sea, with dense forest on the sound side and row on row of dunes on the ocean side, coming to an abrupt halt on a wide, shelly beach. The dunes are like a desert, tawny browns of winter dominating the scraggly grasses. The desolation continues until one reaches the Mullet Pond. The pond is a sudden change from the semi-sterile, barren sands to an eruption of tall swamp grasses and cattails. A shallow, brackish pool, filled with countless tiny minnows, the air alive with the talk of birds, is surrounded by thick forest that has emerged from the sweetness and fertility of an ancient swamp. Tracks of birds, horses, sheep, and small animals are everywhere, for this is their refuge.

Along the sound side of Shackleford Banks a few graveyards mark the sites of villages abandoned nearly a century ago. Virtually no sign is left of the homes. The few bricks and broken dishes scattered the length of the island are about all that remains. The largest and best known community was Diamond City, named, it is said, for the black and white diamond shapes identifying Cape Lookout Light. The village was all but destroyed by hurricanes in the late 1890s.

Not far from the Mullet Pond a portion of a cedar fence, hand carved, marks one burial ground, still sheltered by trees that have resisted salt and storm. Mosses and lichens identify this as a humid climate. An occasional cedar headstone has stood the test of time, as have simple stones marking head and foot of most graves. Nearly all are lost in the tangles of thorny smilax vines and sprawling, distorted trees, silent witnesses to a different way of life. Shackleford was gradually being deserted in the last of the 19th century, and by 1915 was totally abandoned by its inhabitants, who had moved to Harkers Island, Salterpath, and Ricepath on Bogue Banks, and to Morehead City's Promise Land. Though abandoned, these little burial grounds are not forgotten. A haven of silence except for the soughing of wind in the treetops and the chatter of birds, this is a relief from roar of ocean and whistle of cold nor'west wind. These are the maritime woods, now at peace. All too soon they will be tick- and chigger-infested, alive with flies, gnats, and mosquitoes in the stifling heat of next summer.

When we walked back to the inner beach, we looked with affection at our boat, lying at anchor a short distance offshore, rolling in the chop. The rest of our party had fired up a charcoal grill. The fragrance of sizzling hamburgers, the sound of drink bottles and cans being opened, seemed inconsistent. Here should be the smells of the sea, of mullet sputtering on an open fire, of clams steaming. There should be the tang of oysters, the crumbling goodness of cornbread, the fragrance of yaupon tea. I could visualize the old-timer in rubber boots, nets drying in the sun, wife in gingham bonnet and long skirt cooking up the vittles, the iron washpot, the overturned skiff. Both would be lean and tanned and hard, with a deep understanding of natural mysteries. Inside their modest cottage, nailed to the wall, would be an Outer Banks calendar, a length of cotton twine onto which seven hand-carved gum root net floats had been threaded. With one float tied off so it couldn't slide, the others draped from a sccond nail, a float would be advanced each day until today, the Lord's Day, when all seven floats hung together.

Dishes were scarce in those days, and were usually reserved for special occasions. By the water keg should rest the work-a-day cup, a conch shell. Conchs (whelks) are of two types, left-handed and right-handed. From such a mug, according to preference, many a cup of yaupon tea was drunk, after simmering to strength over a drift-wood-fired stove. Conchs served as multi-purpose tools. Besides being drinking vessels, blowing horns, flower pots, and gardening tools, they had still another use. Called Bahama mittens, they were unexcelled in a fight. Along with a few net weights, they could relieve the monotony of many a Saturday night in town. I was not so deep in reverie as to miss the first call to hamburgers, hot and juicy off a twentieth-century grill. It even seemed diplomatic to accept ice in my low-calorie drink.

~~~~~~~~~~~~~~~~~~~~~~~~~~~~~~~

Although in winter the tourists are gone from the shore, the regular residents remain active. A possum that lived in the woods just beyond our house had been raiding the hen house. We don't keep hens, but if we did that's where they'd be. Actually, he was attracted by the sweet smell of McIntosh apples hanging overhead in the net house. It was either possum or apples, so I set a trap for him, and one night I caught him.

First we heard the dog yapping. She has three types of yap: one means that she has something cornered that she feels safe in cornering; another means she's not so sure of her own safety; the last is a soaring scream of full panic. This summons was a simple "Yap!" Sure enough, there was a possum in the live trap.

To show how far things have deteriorated, ever since a recent governor quit the possum market has been declining. No matter where we asked, we couldn't get any possum takers, even when we offered to throw in the recipe. Either no one was hungry, or tastes have changed. I asked the fellow driving the garbage truck. No suh! He wasn't eatin' no possum. Then I tried a couple of sports at one of the marine labs. No way, man! They went back to counting fish scales. The gas station attendant just gave me a blank stare.

Things didn't appear very promising, so we headed for the woods that evening, stopping on a dirt road to drop Brer Possum out of the bag in what we deemed a suitable neighborhood. We watched him turn and waddle down a ditch, making a bee line in the direction from which we'd just transported him. We got back in the car and headed for home, hoping to get there before the bad penny returned. Then a double take: our possum had changed course and was heading east again! Seconds later we realized that there were two possums, both making time in opposite directions. It was a busy roadside.

Next morning, talking to Ken Newsom, I learned that, while he hadn't yet nabbed the fox raiding his chicken coop Down East, he too had caught a big possum. He had brought it back to the west side of the river and turned it loose, figuring that there was just as much for it to eat to the west'ard as in his chicken yard. One can't help picturing heavy possum traffic around here. I can see it now, two possums meeting.

"Howdy pardner! Where do you hail from?"

"Wiregrass Community. Where y'all from?"

"Hull Swamp. Just got transferred."

"How 'bout that! So did I. Was there last week—easy pickins, huh?"

"Yeah man. Get to see a lot of country in this business."

Meanwhile, eastbound cars with possums are meeting westbound cars with possums, and the possum population is getting real mixed up. Can't hardly tell a Yankee from a Southerner any more. There must be a moral here, and surely there is a future. I'm considering applying for a research grant to study possum migration. I'm told that Dr. Al Chestnut over at the University published a paper on clam migration, so I figure to do it on marsupials, even though the market is depressed.

~~~~~~~~~~~~~~~~~~~~~~

One human creature that does frequent the shore in winter is the duck hunter. It's a well-known fact that duck hunters are crazy. They have to be to get up before decently getting to sleep, to go forth and make themselves miserable. When the weather seems impossible—cold and rainy, with the wind blowing in icy reaches across the water—duck hunting is at its best.

The trouble is that duck hunters don't come to their senses until it's too late to turn back. I recall a particular hunt I joined a few years ago. We set out from Don Morris' camp late one afternoon, bound for Core Banks. Not until we'd rounded the shelter of a lee to come face-to-face with a bitter nor'west wind screeching down Core Sound did the thought occur to me, What am I doing here? Frost-flecked waves slammed the bow, sending icy salt water flying as we wallowed towards the Banks.

Core Banks in winter is cold, windswept, desolate. The beach is flat and bare, and a back-eddying surf was rolling in. Wave crests picked up by the wind were whipped back seaward. Sand, scouring across shell-littered flats, had piled into windrows, and old sand fences were a jumble beneath tufts of beach grass. We selected bunks in one of the fishing shacks clustered in the meager lee of the dunes and began preparations for hunting. The companionship was superb:

jokes flying, coffee steaming, long tales of past hunts and great dogs, duck and goose calls squawking, straight-faced lies dispensed as solemn truths. Despite plans for early rising, the hours melted away before the last nimrod reluctantly gave in to sleep.

It was bitter cold and dark as, half-awake, we fumbled into long johns, insulated underwear, heavy wool socks, several pairs of woolen trousers, sweaters, sweat shirts, wool shirts, ponchos, gloves, mittens, parkas, coveralls, waders, and rain suits. Scarcely able to stagger, we loaded ourselves further with guns, ammunition, decoys, handwarmers, and other paraphernalia essential to the modern hunter, to set off into the raw darkness.

Some went to offshore blinds, some to exposed points, others to dunes on the sound side to ambush the wily waterfowl if it strayed near. Gibbie Smith and I chose a wind-ridden point that was sparsely covered with weather-worn and bedraggled beach grass, and set out decoys. I snugged down behind a wisp of grass and rolled up in a camouflage poncho to watch the night turn to morning. Water slapped on the beach a dozen feet away, wind whistled in the grass, and, as the day grew, the chill increased slowly. First the fingers, next the toes, and then the cold was creeping in everywhere, like water penetrating a sponge.

A red sun lifted from the ocean to reach across the dunes, but the temperature continued to fall. The decoys, tossing a few yards away, became glassy with ice as they dipped and rolled. Salt water met wind and congealed. The white foam of the shoreline began to grow, with ice clinging to stems of grasses and brush, and the wind cut deeper. A great vee of geese passed down the sound, barking. The morning patrol of gulls rose and fell like a floating necklace in their hovering and soaring. The early light glistened red and yellow from their pale feathers.

I was numb but still hopeful, pulling the poncho closer and flexing my chill-stiffened muscles. The sun rose higher, maybe twenty degrees above the horizon. Not a bird within range. Visions of hot coffee, a warm fire, and breakfast became irresistible. We gave in and started the long trudge back, almost immobilized by the cold. Camp seemed miles away.

From the dock far ahead, Franc White was waving wildly. I looked around to see that a flight was skimming the ground, heading directly at us. With no place to hide, I dropped to the mud, trying to get the gun in position. Just a few yards out of range the flight veered, and we could see the white face markings of brant. We had muffed it. Tear-streaked, red-faced, and numb, we stumbled into the shack where the others waited, also empty-handed, telling one another of the birds they'd seen and missed. Country ham, cheese and onion omelet, hot coffee, and fried potatoes consoled and gave us hope.

Next morning we chose a blind not two hundred yards offshore, but a mile distant by a tortuous branch-marked channel. The boat pitched and slammed, and solid sheets of water sluiced over us. The icing salt burned our cheeks, and our eyes streamed tears. The blind looked lonely on the vast, wind-lashed sound. Freezing spray fingered its way into every crack and seam, soaking my gloves. I was sitting in a pool of ice water.

Clumsily, we put our gear aboard the blind, climbed into it from the tossing skiff, closed the door, and watched with mixed emotions as the boat wound its way among the decoys and skipped lightly across the white-streaked black waters. The eastern horizon was beginning to lighten, silhouetting the island, bleak as ever.

The blinds were constructed somewhat like open-topped privies on pilings, four to six feet above the water. The walls were just high enough to give protection from the biting winds and keep the seated hunter out of sight of sharp-eyed ducks and geese. Low enough to shoot over when standing, the walls had one-inch by eighteen-inch slots about a foot from the top for peering out without showing oneself. Inside, we stuffed our gear wherever we could. Then, "I guess we oughta look for some ducks." The idea was no longer as appealing as it had been.

I peered through one slot, studying the still-dark waters, where the ice-glazed decoys were bobbing under a sky now starless. Far off, a flight of geese moved in a ragged vee and disappeared over the horizon. Through another slot I saw even less. Then, turning to the north opening, wide-eyed to search the half-light, I jerked back in shock: my eyeballs had iced up in a split second. I didn't dare blink, or even try to roll my eyes, for fear of shattering them. It was as if a CO^2 bottle had been discharged in my face. Numb, blinded by streaming tears, I knew that any duck that approached from that direction was safe. Shivering deeper into my heavy clothing, I could understand why duck hunters have to be a little crazy.

While we awaited rescue from the blind, thoughts of a cruise south were nudging me again. Ducks go south in this weather, I reasoned, so why shouldn't we? The Intracoastal Waterway, familiar yet always new, beckoned, and strongly. Surely it was time for Mary and me to be snowbirds once more.

~~~~~~~~~~~~~~~~~~~~~~~~

Tucked into the tail end of the year are recollections of Christmas, a succession of events over the decades. I guess it has been man's busiest season ever since ancient times. We are coming up on the Moon of the Long Night, in far northern Eskimo lands a season of seemingly everlasting darkness. Only the light of stars and moon reflects off the glittering blue-silver ice fields that stretch from horizon to horizon. It is claimed that ancients became worried about the gods of darkness taking over and got busy doing something to revive the gods of light. Before the birth of Christ there was a celebration to recognize the end of the shortening days and the start of a new year. When one sees the sun ending its southward wandering and easing slowly north, it all makes sense. The Moon of the Long Night is the full moon closest to December 21. It may occur as early as December 7 or as late as January 4. When the sun has reached twenty-three degrees south declination, it leaves but ten hours of daylight in Carolina.

A northwest American Indian tradition said that the more a man gave, the greater he was. Great leaders were known to divest themselves of everything they had, to prove to themselves that it was they, not their material goods, that made them great. But it was also a sign of being a lesser person to refuse a gift, so, in order to maintain one's reputation, one must exceed the gift received. Visualize, if you will, a bunch of stripped-down Indians trying to get rid of the last breech-clout to prove themselves the best. This is potlatch.

Thoughts of Indians always recall Christmas in the Dakotas. Frigid winds howled across barren hills. Sweeping snow hid gravel roads beneath a white blanket while we rammed snowdrifts, trying to get to the grandfolks' place for Christmas. Granddad in snow-white beard handed out presents during a time when no one could afford them. Handblown glass ornaments on the tree gleamed in the wavering candlelight. Granddad had a shining brass fire extinguisher sitting next to the tree, and he was always in the room when the candles were burning. In the next room the dining table groaned with the incredible delights that Grandmother, Mother, and aunts had removed from the big Monarch wood range. There have never been bigger turkeys.

One wartime Christmas was spent outdoors—walking post; another, yachting—aboard a minesweeper. The ship rocked in the swell, the tree above the table swayed as I savored the first good meal in months, only to experience the agony of losing it from seasickness. Then home, married and living aboard *Silver Spray*, anchored in Peltier Creek, Christmas with a small juniper alight in the cabin. The old Shipmate wood stove glowed, giving dry warmth. We watched ducks paddle by and otters playing and watching ducks, too, then rowed ashore to visit landsmen.

And oh, yes! there was that Christmas in Martinique, as guests of a poor but proud French-speaking family. Our guide had insisted. Each course was accented by an appropriate wine. But for the Americans, a bottle of Scotch, because all Americans preferred Scotch. Songs of Christmas in two languages, and toasts: the grandfather toasting the Americans, "who came unselfishly to our aid when the great hurricane struck, and again when Mt. Pelée erupted, with food, medicine, and shelter." Then the father toasted the Americans who had freed Paris from the Hun and fed Europe with the Hoover plan.

The son praised Americans for freedom from the Nazis, and his wife reminded him of the Marshall plan. Not to be outdone, two French sailors praised Americans—and New York's pretty girls. When we left the island in pre-dawn hours, the porter, unabashed at having to work on a holiday, stood in the middle of the runway, songbook in hand, lustily singing French carols.

We baked Christmas chicken in our folding Coleman oven in the Everglades, were caught by Christmas fervor in New Orleans' French Quarter, camped among saguaros and chollas in the desert southwest, with coyotes for carolers. The worst of Christmas is to be caught between here and there and to spend it in a motel with nothing to do.

In a sense, the New Year has already begun. The winter solstice has passed, but a beat in the pulse of time. It is a new season. Wisely, the ancients felt it proper to declare this a time of holy days. Perhaps this is why the Lord found the time appropriate for sending a messenger. How could Christmas fit, say, in midsummer? No, it had to be at the beginning of the newest year.

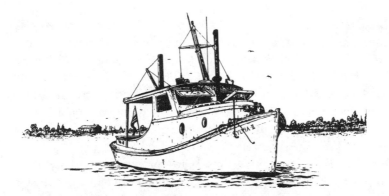

BITTERSWEET WATERS
SOUTHWARD

To the saltwater fisherman or sailor, sweet waters are fresh and salt water is bitter brine. In the estuaries and the intracoastal water- ways the bitter and sweet waters intermingle.

To accomplish a major expedition, there must be a great deal of planning, even conniving, such as first convinc- ing an otherwise normal wife-type female that fishing is a great treat, a pleasure, a joy. Then if you succeed in such a ruse, the next hurdle to overcome is that of faraway places when wife is in a frame of mind to stay at home. This can be achieved best, not by further mention of fishing, but by romanticizing. So speak not of Mepps lures or Orvis flyrods, but whisper of sundowns in secluded lagoons, of moon over sparkling waters, of lazying in the sun beneath swaying palms (even swaying moss will do), of oranges and bananas and passion fruit, of warm beaches and paradise in the tropics.

Though the theory is flawless, my wife's response was neither reluctant approval nor flat-footed disapproval. Instead, she floored me with, "You know, our boat is getting rather old, and she's never been to Florida. Why don't we take her down to Marjorie Kinnan Rawlings' country—you know, Cross Creek and the St. Johns? I think *Sylvia* would like that." That woman had stolen my thunder! She had taken over. But I rallied and made a firm decision: this trip, especially as it would be by boat, would not start on a Friday. Any sailor will agree that it is not superstition, but fact. Yes, I really put my foot down then and there.

This river that we—that is, my wife—proposed to cruise flows north. Now a north-flowing river is not your everyday river. Just a few perverse rivers insist on flowing north, instead of the tried, true, and traditional south. What comes to mind first is the Nile in Egypt. After that, most of us stall out. Greatest of all is the Red River of the North, because it rises near where I was born in North Dakota and waggles up to Hudson's Bay. And the St. Johns, too, is one of those contrary rivers where upstream is down or downstream is up, depending on which way you're paddling. In any case, it has a reputation for great bass fishing, and that was indeed one of my ulterior motives.

The very best times are autumn and spring. Autumn having already bowed out, we drew up a hasty packing list: stuff bags for clothing, sleeping bags, and other personal gear, all to be slung in hammocks made from scraps of a trawl net; the twenty-year-old Coleman stove from the car, three five-gallon tins of fresh water, and—most important—fresh water fishing tackle. We lashed the Avon inflatable atop the cockpit canopy and hung over the coaming an aging, even decrepit, Sea Gull outboard borrowed from George Brandt, retired mule mechanic. A big wrench was adequate for altering its frozen condition.

By now it was rather late in the day, and a cold north wind was blowing more than briskly across the sound. The tide was beginning to flood, and my brother and his wife were standing around waiting to wish us bon voyage. Mary and I had a hasty consultation and agreed that we might as well get underway. After a quick flurry with last-minute gear, we relinquished custody of our cottage to Susan and Bill, started the engine, and tied *Sylvia II* loose. Long ago we'd learned about using the tide to our advantage. Local boatmen have an adage for the southbound: tie on a stern anchor and when the bow swings the direction you want to go, tie her loose. The last of the flood through Beaufort Inlet would push us down Bogue Sound until we caught the ebb of Bogue Inlet, giving us the advantage of one or two knots. Riding the ebb down the Cape Fear River would lead to a fair current down the Waccamaw. All together such free rides would save us considerably through Georgia.

Despite our many previous waterway trips with *Silver Spray*, there was still a small feeling of apprehension, of excitement. With sweaty hands I swung the bow into the channel and noted the time as we passed Milepost 212, as the distance designated by the Corps of Engineers from Norfolk. Only then did we realize that we were at last underway, for better, for worse. A load was beginning to lift. We slipped past summer homes and camps and barren spoil islands. The sound was deserted except for an occasional crabber working the shallows. At the village of Swansboro the swift currents of Bogue Inlet tugged at us. The sun was low when we passed the great Marine Base on New River. Orderly rows of amphibious tractors lined the bank, their crews securing them for the night.

The wind was still fresh, and cold. Darkness was approaching rapidly when a narrow channel at the north end of Topsail Island offered a possible anchorage. In the fading light we nosed *Sylvia II* into the quieter backwater. We circled like a dog preparing for retiring, while the depth indicator flashed assurances. I lowered the anchor into the darkening waters, and Mary backed slightly until the hook bit hard into the mud. A little surge of power to set it firmly, and she shut down the engine. Our only company, besides two milk jugs buoying crab pots, was a gathering of oyster catchers in a row on a little spoil island where tufts of grasses had grown up among sea-scoured shells. There was virtual silence, the wind sighing slightly, the lap and burble of waves sweeping by on a flooding tide, the reassuring groan of the anchor line.

Supper was also burbling by the time we sat out on the weather deck, not too weary from our first day to watch the stars appear. A heavily rolling surf rumbled and moaned ashore on the narrow strand that separated us from the ocean. The engine heat from a day's running warmed the cabin, the gimbaled lamp glowed softly, and we couldn't help wondering how in the world we could be so lucky: forever chasing rainbows, trying to catch a falling star. As the engine cooled, so did the cabin, and sleeping bags felt good.

I'd been sleeping soundly when I became aware of the hatch cover opening. Startled, I sat up to see Mary standing in the open hatch, star gazing. She'd decided to check the anchor after the tide changed and was struck by the brilliance of the night. Scorpio seemed to be hanging from the sky, apart from all the rest. No painter, no photographer could capture its beauty. Only the heart could remember.

The anchor was up with the sunrise, and we felt our way past the birds on their shoal to thread a route through the marshes to the main channel. "Hold her 'bout south, mate," I ordered, and settled back with my coffee to admire ospreys on a channel marker watching us go by. In the yard of one home a pair of kids was waiting for the school bus to gather them in.

Boating is as much an attitude as a physical thing. As children we read that "there is nothing like messing around in boats." As adults we heard a friend remark that he had always been "boat-poor." It has taken a while, but we are beginning to understand that we are in the same condition. In the course of many years of experience and observation, we have come to categorize boatmen. One type is forever in a hurry and wants the machine—his boat—somehow to resemble a torpedo, long and low and extremely powerful. He who may idolize Hemingway would want a sport boat, one with long poles bristling, some meant to snag fish, others meant to spread the word about snagging fish. A real giveaway is the boatman with flybridge upon flybridge. Myself, I'm afraid of high places. Then there's the fashion seeker, who requires the latest model, for decorating with bikini beauties. The upkeep is tremendous, though today you can buy a boat on a credit card, so you don't have to ask how much. There are the loners, too, forever trying to sail around the world single-handed, and making it sometimes. Finally, the rest of us, dumb but happy, keep poking into back bays and hidden harbors, just messing around in boats.

As for the Intracoastal Waterway, it is a way of life neither of the sea nor of the land, a meandering through a series of rivers, sounds, cuts, and canals that connect the inland waters of the east coast and Gulf. Having cruised this route many times, to do it again after a lapse of several years is like returning home to see old friends and renew old memories, scenes of mystery and history, of romance and adventure, like old plantations and rice fields, manor houses and the gracious living of a time when cotton was king. The course is through mile after mile of otters watching from beneath the brown grasses that overhang the banks; deer standing on shore, half-hidden by thick vines; egrets and herons probing muddy shores; scaups and buffleheads flushing in splashing takeoff and rush of beating wings; and pelicans soaring solemnly in undulating formation over mirror-calm bays.

Cities and towns clutter the shores here and there, each different from the last; yet all seaports are kin. Along river banks aging summer homes sagged, their rickety piers decaying. At oil docks and fish houses shrimp boats and trawlers rafted, rust-streaked and weathered of hull, masts and decks a confusion of nets, brightly colored floats, and chafing gear. Sportsfishing fleets, at rest after a long, hard season of charters, fancier than the work boats, yet less flashy than the private pleasure craft.

Cruising with George Brandt on *Ilanwomon* a few years before, we'd had to tie up for repairs—it was Friday the 13th—in Southport, North Carolina. In a café grim-faced fishermen clustered about the radio turned to full volume. Against the crackling sounds of the voices of searchers for survivors of a lost fishing boat, their unshaven compatriots discussed the chances—sixteen hours in icy waters—not a hope of a man's surviving, even in a life jacket. The heat would be sucked out of the body. Yet that Tommy always was a tough one. Coffee and cigarettes were faint comfort to the men ashore. Men of iron, but each feeling a knife in his vitals. Then a transmission hushed the voices: "Two picked up alive . . . floating in a fish box." A tall graybeard let out a whoop and slammed a comrade across the back, sending coffee and cigarette ashes flying. The small café swelled with cheering. Faces brightened and light-hearted joking revealed the extent of their concern. Two of their kind had survived.

The Waccamaw River was layered with undulating ribbons of fog that hid the tea-colored water. The boat seemed adrift in cotton. Trees were monsters emerging from the whiteness. Then, with Georgetown, South Carolina, in sight, the wind and rain moved in, slashing across the bay. The cold dampness penetrated, the paper mill smelled, oil and grease in iridescent flecks slid out of the harbor on an ebbing tide, along with bits of garbage. On the little Sampit River tugboats squatted morosely at dockside, dark and abandoned. Upriver, ocean-going ships under glaring floodlights were taking on cargo.

All night the rain tapped steadily on the decks. Morning was only the lightening of lead-gray skies. Yellow foul weather gear glinted with the wetness, and rain splashed on the open deck as we took the flood tide through canals and winding rivers. We passed the day meeting loaded barges and straining tugs on blind river bends, taking a rolling from the wake of an energy-guzzling yacht when its roaring engines slammed walls of water against the banks of a narrow cut. Then mile upon mile of Cape Romain Migratory Bird Refuge slid by, bought and paid for by American hunters so that ducks and geese, oyster catchers and ospreys can live and perpetuate the wild-life heritage that belongs to all Americans.

Swift tidal currents tilted the buoys to seaward as our boat struggled against the racing tide across the ship channels of Charleston harbor. The green and gray lump of Fort Sumter recalled the smoke and pain and agony of brother against brother failing to understand themselves, while on the Battery the still-fashionable homes of another era stood shoulder to shoulder. Then the sea of masts where sailboats clustered inside the concrete-walled yacht basin was upon us, the smiles of boating friends recognizing us, the wiping of grease-stained hands as they rose from the holes where faulty engines dwell.

There was a great ocean racer, a sailing machine from a faraway hailing port, swift of lines and beautiful in her merciless efficiency. Her crew was aloof and hard, with the confidence that comes of wealth and power. She stole quietly out of the harbor and headed for open sea, looking for all the world like an angry, straining greyhound being held back by a tight leash.

There are uneventful days on the waterway, and those that are overlong, when the anchorage is still far away at sundown. The sun, setting beneath a limitless sky like a vast, inverted bowl, turns gray clouds to reds and golds. Darkness creeps in from the east, and the flashing of red and white markers begins to show as the light fades. Then come chart reading by subdued light and searching with binoculars for day markers, for shoals lie in wait to trip us. Overhead the stars grow brighter while narrow channels grow narrower. Straining eyes and probing spotlight search for missing guideposts until, at last, security for the night and the reassuring rocking of the boat lets us give in to weariness.

From the anchorage, we left with the rising sun to follow the Beaufort River south. The wind was rising and meeting the ebb tide, standing the waves on end. Streaks of foam marked conflicting currents as Sylvia II sliced through the slop, sending occasional spray in rainbow sheets. Mary went below to dog down the ports and secure the forward hatch cover.

It was our first trip southward with Silver Spray some years back that gave us a beating on exposed inland waters and made believers of us. We'd been following a motor sailer, Swamp Yankee, and she, all sails set, pointed the way across Port Royal Sound south of Beaufort, South Carolina. We paused, but then—if he can do it, why can't we? We began to find out why when the sofa leaped its chocks and slammed across the deckhouse and every bit of loose gear was rolling and tossing. The last straw was when a fire extinguisher jumped its bracket and started squirting, mostly at the helmsman. At least I had something to hang onto until I could get the boat turned around. We sneaked back to the shelter of the Marine Base at Parris Island, to lick wounds and heal pride. It was a three-day blow, but when we did cross the sound, it was in fog and a "slick ca'am." Later we learned that the other boat, skippered by a seasoned, salty Yankee who'd ridden out typhoons in the South Pacific, had by no means escaped unscathed. All canvas had blown out, and the captain had learned about ebb tides and contrary winds in the Old South.

This time Port Royal Sound was more amiable, and *Sylvia II* crossed the open waters with ease, bobbing like a gull, brushing aside the spray and letting the waves hiss and bubble by. We slid along, leaving a widening vee, one side ultimately collapsing on the sea islands for which South Carolina and Georgia are famous, the other meeting and mingling with the sweet water of the wide, deep coastal rivers from which estuaries are born. Even so, only after we'd slid into Skull Creek on the other side did the nervous twitterings of recollection begin to ease. I have always been, and hope always to remain, a fair-weather sailor.

Northbound early one spring, we had nicely entered Beaufort River from Port Royal Sound when, just as the sun was sliding below the horizon, my bird-watching wife picked up the binoculars to see what kind of birds were sitting on some driftwood. They turned out to be the heads of two fishermen, tangled in the lines of their capsized skiff, adrift for several hours in choppy, chilly waters. They were so weak that I had to go overboard myself to cut them loose from a tangle of lines before we could heave and haul them out of the cold river and over the side of our rolling boat. I wasn't aware of being cold when I opened the throttles and raced towards the nearest pier, hoping they would still be alive when we got them ashore, but I do remember the warmth of the stiff whiskey when they were safe and we were tied up for the night. Next morning there was a big basket of fruit from two happy though still waterlogged fishermen.

While boating is more of a mood, an approach to life, than is any other form of recreation, the mood applies to the working boatman as well. Walter Cronkite, an avid yachtsman, believes that boating types are blessed with imagination, that it is the rare skipper who has never fancied, as he casts off, that he has a hold full of tea for Southampton, or oil for the lamps of China. I remember the time we brought a load of coconuts from Miami, for Morehead City delivery. I don't recall what became of them, but if anyone remembers a surplus of coconuts in coastal North Carolina twenty-five years ago, odds are they arrived aboard *Silver Spray*, f.o.b. Miami.

~~~~~~~~~~~~~~~~~~~~~

The waves were running about five feet and sweeping level with the deck as *Sylvia II* plunged on. Storm clouds were building in the north, and the needle on the barometer was dropping like a stone. The wind was freshening, and the seas were growing. Apprehension was growing, too, as the engine began to sputter occasionally, catch up and sputter again. Our thoughts were as black as the horizon. Mary disappeared into the engine room to pat the manifold. "Keep going, now." Georgia is full of bays, sounds, and rivers of every size and description, so we knew it wouldn't be far to a hiding place. The old Carolina fisherman's advice kept coming back: "When it blows, find the lee of a pine tree." We were looking for that pine tree.

Finally, a jut of land and a creek appeared, and against wooded high ground we could see the rigging of shrimpers and the promise of shelter. Though the wind whistled still, everything was suddenly calm. Even the engine seemed to be missing less as we crawled upstream towards the jumble of masts and rigging. Like a compact car amid freight trucks, *Sylvia II* nosed alongside a formidable wooden wall. I yelled up to the head peering down at us, "How 'bout layin' 'longside?" "Sure!" Mary heaved a line, and I put out fenders, secured, and climbed aboard the big trawler, outermost of several rafted together.

"Where ya from?" A hefty, sun-bronzed man was eyeing me with some suspicion, as were two more who were mending a net. "North Carolina." "Oh! Well, that's okay. We tie up at Stumpy Point. Those folks treat us real well. If you're from North Carolina, you must be okay." We were in, thanks to some nice folks at Stumpy Point. This was King shrimp docks, five miles from the village of Valona. One of the skippers made a call, and it wasn't long before a mechanic arrived with parts, but meanwhile there was a tour of the fleet.

Now *Sylvia II* began her career as a commercial fishing boat and had a good reputation, but we looked at a new boat that had everything. Completely modern, she was equipped with air conditioning, stereo, radar, autopilot, plush crew's quarters, deep freezes, fancy galley. Then the skipper demonstrated the latest device, a shipboard computer that takes over when you tell it where you want to fish. It allows for wind drift, figures all angles. If there is a snag, it dodges it. The trawler was so modern that I began to doubt the need for captain and crew. In a few years perhaps someone will push a button, and the boat will go out and fish while the crew sits ashore, sipping mint juleps or slipping peanuts in their cokes. Still, I wondered, can a computer mend a net? Maybe technological perfection will be the net that never needs mending.

Engine repairs made, we cast off, bound for a sleepy creek backed up by live oaks where we could drop anchor. Anchoring out is seldom practiced by large yachts and many so-called "boaters," but for us it's the best way to go. Stop early in an attractive cove or creek away from traffic, lean back and watch the landscape change as tide or wind dictates. Listen to the birds, watch the sunset and the terns in their last frenzied feeding, the shorebirds assembling on their resting grounds. Put over hook and line and take the risk that trout, blue, or sea mullet may furnish supper. Then, when evening stars come out, see how the world spins.

That night we turned on the anchor light, on the unlikely chance that another boat might wander by. We turned in to the sounds of water lapping and anchor line complaining in the chock. It was so quiet that we went to sleep at once. Around midnight or later two boats sped by. Scarcely had their wakes subsided when a searchlight covered us in an explosion of light, then snapped off. The third boat went its way, and we drifted back to sleep. A day or two later we heard on the radio about a big drug bust. Apparently our quiet anchorage had been a rendezvous point. All around us had been feds and revenuers, smugglers and pirates—this was a sleepy creek?

∾∾∾∾∾∾∾∾∾∾∾∾∾∾∾∾

A trip that is a matter of a day or so by automobile hurtling across bridges and along four-laned asphalt trails, and but two or three hours by giant jets rumbling and leaving contrails across the sky, we can easily stretch into weeks. But car and plane are capsuled in another world, while we are in the reality of the open air, accompanied by hungry gulls soaring hopefully above our wake. Disappointed, they bank gracefully to join their brethren on a salt-washed shelly shore, until another boat passes and stirs their hopes again. Now and then we hear the snort of a porpoise as it cruises alongside to inspect our bow wake. Rolling an eye curiously at the odd critters standing above, it smiles its imperturbable smile before descending into murky green waters to see what kind of fish might be waiting to be caught as a mid-morning snack.

Anchored in the wind-tossed Frederica River, near the ruins of the ancient fort that was the dream of General James Oglethorpe 250 years ago, there was time to think of these things. We were protected from a howling nor'west wind by vast marshes on one side, and, should the wind shift, by a stand of magnificent live oaks, streamers of Spanish moss standing out from their limbs. I'm not sure that it's dreams of cargo, as Walter Cronkite suggests. It seems more like the cow looking over the fence at greener grass. Folks who cruise are seeking a new Shangri-La, while trying to escape the realities of Utopia.

An inescapable reality is the crab pot. Crab pots are the bane of boatmen. Crabbers set their pots on the edge of deep water, but currents, the wash of boats, and other phenomena seem invariably to set a half-dozen or so in the channel. The buoys, usually plastic jugs or clusters of corks attached to the pots by rope, bob there, waiting to be snatched by a passing propeller blade and wound securely, pots and all, around the shaft, to the accompaniment of great thumpings and bangings. Dodging the floats, lining up ranges, following twisting channels, we eased past Golden Isles settlements and landings, eyeing those beautiful islands being purchased by oil-wealthy Arabs with used American dollars, developed by Americans into vacation homes for the wealthy of all nations, leaving the local poor a little poorer. Unchanged are the big tides, often five, sometimes more than ten feet, causing currents to run strong and scour channels deep. Those who misjudge are still left high and dry on a mudbank.

∽∽∽∽∽∽∽∽∽∽∽∽∽

We cruised into a different world when we crossed the St. Marys River into Florida. It's a psychological thing as well, for everyone wants to start basking in the sunshine. No matter how cold, or how dim the sun, on the day of crossing into Florida, they begin stripping down to the bare necessities. Florida, you must understand, is a magic state of mind where fish always bite and pretty girls lounge under every palm tree. Though it was sloppy weather when we reached the Land of Sunshine, relative quiet prevailed when we turned to our next anchorage on the Ft. George River. Nearby, a solitary elderly man sat fishing from his skiff. We gave a friendly wave while circling, trying to find the perfect spot. Agreeing on the site, I dropped the hook and Mary shut down the engine.

The old man seemed to be having some luck, so I delved into the tackle box, studying each lure. The water was fast and deep. A heavy lure was in order. Though I couldn't see what the other man was catching, clearly these were trout waters. I'd try a jig, maybe a bucktail, or a plastic unknown. I thrashed water, changed lures and retrieved nothing but grass, while the old man continued to boat fish after fish.

By sundown he'd had enough. He wound up his motor, upped anchor and came alongside, introducing himself, "I'm a retired railroad man who's seen the light." A pause, then, "See you aren't getting anything." I agreed. He pointed, "Got a couple hundred dollars worth right over there where the Lord told me to try." "If you'll ask the Lord proper-like and use shelled whole shrimp, the Lord will provide some bull whiting." He passed over a fistful of shrimp. Mary had been listening without comment. As the fisherman turned to start his motor, she suggested, "Why don't you give the Lord a hand and fasten your life jacket?" He smiled, wrestled with the fastenings, then, "I've seen the light and hope you will, too," and he roared off into the sunset.

Sure enough, I tried the shrimp like he said and within five minutes we, too, were blessed with bending rod and protesting fish. We were not familiar with "bull" whiting, though we've caught many a sea mullet. These were averaging eighteen inches and close to two pounds. The rain set in, lashing the river to a foggy haze. Sailboats anchored nearby were dipping and bobbing, the howling wind rattling their rigging, but on board *Sylvia II* all was bliss. With the sweet smell of sea mullet frying was the fresh fragrance of coffee bubbling in a somewhat leaky pot. While we waited for the storm to subside, I couldn't help thinking of the warm-hearted old man, "Fish wherever the Lord tells you and use the right bait. Things will work out."

∾∾∾∾∾∾∾∾∾∾∾∾∾∾

Jacksonville is the place you swear you'll never get to if you leave the Intracoastal at Mayport when the tide is ebbing. It should be a historic moment, being at the mouth of the River May, as it was once called. If the tide is flooding it seems more historic. If the river traffic is not heavy, you can enjoy sightseeing the big ships and shipments, the floating drydocks. It is hard to imagine that where high rises soar and deep-draft vessels cruise was once known as Cow Crossing. We berthed at Graham's—now Lamb's—Boat Yard on the Ortega River west of Jacksonville. The Ortega stands for boating in Jacksonville: the Grahams were there for three generations, and the famous Huckins yard is there.

After spending some time in Jacksonville, exploring the old riverfront and the possibilities for making Mary's pilgrimage to Cross Creek, we decided to get underway to Palatka. When you leave the shelter of the Ortega, you enter a portion of the St. Johns that seems more lake than river. The weather started out not the best, nor yet the worst, but we figured on plenty of hidey-holes along the way. Well, it got worse, and it got tiresome, too. And that's how we found Trout Creek and the good feeling that comes from finding a welcome when you come out of foul weather into a safe harbor and discover your kind of people.

A surging wind was rolling up big waves, and rows of whitecaps marched across the dark murkiness. *Sylvia II* was performing well, but spray fogged the windshield so that we could scarcely see the ominous-looking round floats of crab pots that lurked in the troughs. Wherever we looked it was like crossing a mine field. The thought of one wrapped around the propeller in this weather wasn't exactly comforting. Finding relief at last in the shelter of a cove, we picked up the creek entrance. At its mouth Trout Creek is wide and deep, with only a thin bulwark of waterlilies, grasses, and brush to separate the boatman from the swamps beyond, the tall water maples and cypresses, the tupelos and, occasionally, a lonesome pine or two clinging with dampened roots to a tuft of high ground.

Here the water was only lightly ruffled by the wind. Idling down, an eye on the fathometer, we poked along, hoping for a good anchorage. We rounded a sharp bend and spied a great white yacht just ahead. One of the old style, dating back to the 1920s, *Jane Lee* was long, slim, and handsome, with satiny varnish and gleaming white paint. As we passed, a side door popped open, and a tall, lanky man, sunburned, a long cigar in his mouth, stepped out, joined by a good-looking woman waving cordially. They beckoned us alongside the dock—"plenty of room"—and I'd met my new fishing instructor.

After fishing from Florida to Alaska and from Mexico to Labrador, not always successfully, I find it increasingly clear that exposure to water and fishing rods is only a small part of it. Some folks keep making the same mistakes over and over, and to the local specialist, we can assume, it's rather amusing to watch grayling tactics attempted for spots, or the walleye approach for bass. Hugh Epps, a retired teacher, is a master boat restorer and fisherman, one of the gentleman class, who appreciates the quality and simplicity of the good life. He was still restoring the interior of *Jane Lee*. She had been, as best he and Marie could learn, a commuter boat on the Hudson River, built by a maker of race boats. The result is the comfort and elegance of a baronial estate and the cleanness of line of a thoroughbred. Equipped with the original engine, she is a masterpiece of beauty and efficiency.

But Hugh doesn't use her as a fish boat; a small tender takes the abuse of fishing. The purpose of *Jane Lee* is to take them places so that they can use the little boat. To be sure, they could have bought a trailer and driven here and there, but that involves highways, hotels, feeling rushed or obligated to return home occasionally. They've no such dilemmas; during fishing season they live aboard and go where the fish are: the Keys, or Georgia; up some river or far inland on the St. Johns; sometimes the Gulf. What makes the difference is that Marie likes the boat, the whole idea, and is a topnotch fisherman, too.

Disdaining stiff rods and heavy lines, Hugh considers a medium light rod with fifteen-pound line more than adequate to subdue anything of ten to fifteen pounds if one knows how to fish. If it gets away—after all, it is supposed to be a sport, isn't it? Laying a lure next to a grassy bed surrounded by lilies, I waited until a swirl absorbed the line, then heaved back to set the hook. The lure pulled out of the fish's mouth. Hugh explained that wasn't the way, and proceeded to demonstrate. I tried again: the same furious boil— pause—set the hook. The fight was on. Standing in the rocking boat, rod sharply arched, line slicing the water, it was just as I had always dreamed—a monster! It wouldn't give.

Darkness set in. I could see the white spray flying against the inkiness of woods and water. It was even bigger than I'd thought. Diving deep, the lunker could scarcely be turned away from an escape route through fallen logs. The line hummed a vibrato, hissing as it cut past our anchor line. Hugh sat and smiled and puffed his cigar. I admit I did a superb job of handling that fish. When it reluctantly came to the end I knew it would be a record. In the shadows I judged its size, four feet easily, well, maybe three. Then Hugh caught the line, lifted it until a long snout came out of the water. He snipped the line and said nothing. My world record bass had turned out to be a gar. If only I hadn't seen it before he cut the line, I'd have had a real fish story to tell. Hugh says it was closer to eighteen inches, but he lies.

∾∾∾∾∾∾∾∾∾∾∾∾∾∾∾∾

Not many miles south of Trout Creek stands the great ditch-diggers' dream, the Cross-Florida Barge Canal, the pot of gold for local development interests, financed by the taxpayers. Contractors dug for nearly a dozen years, altering rivers, draining lakes, building reservoirs, clearing land, dispossessing a few families. When the Nixon administration called a halt after learning how critical was the fresh water supply and what would be the ultimate effect, the action was roundly cursed.

We cruised up towards the massive locks that stand at the end of a long, straight canal. Tying up to dolphins, we heard a mechanical voice come through the hailer with its Florida accent intact, asking if we wanted to be locked through. "No, just looking." The water was beginning to boil out, millions of gallons gushing through immense pipes for several minutes. Then silence. Soon the great doors, each as big as a many-storied house, began to swing open, so awesome that we were expecting a fanfare of trumpets. We watched, fascinated, while a tiny—possibly sixteen-foot—outboard boat emerged on a raft of hyacinths, bulling its way through. The operator revved up, waved a beer can at us, and disappeared down the cut.

The multi-million-dollar locks let through, according to the log, a hundred-odd outboard motorboats a month, to go fishing in the multi-million-dollar reservoir above. A manned and staffed monstrosity, it is waiting, in inimitable bureaucratic fashion, for the ships that never come. Yet pressure is on to continue the digging, for to the diggers food and lives mean nothing. After all, like the builders of many other great dams, who are they to care about the people who live there? Mary, looking down on that sea of hyacinths, began to have second thoughts about taking *Sylvia II* to Cross Creek. By the time we reached the Oklawaha, so choked with hyacinths that the mouth of the river was barely identifiable, she had abandoned the idea.

Our boat had accumulated a number of admirers along the way. A young dockmaster in Beaufort, South Carolina, asked for the plans that Mike Alford had drawn. On a winding route through Georgia marshes, we were meeting a shrimper when the skipper popped out of the wheelhouse to snap a picture with his Instamatic. "I sure do like her lines!" And he sure had made our day. In an anchorage off the St. Johns a big fast Huckins idled up one afternoon just to look us over. There were pretty girls and their admirers all over the foredeck. They paid us no mind, but the captain, in spotless white with gold braid on his cap, had eyes only for little *Sylvia II*.

Only once did an old boat lover chase us by automobile: we'd hardly tied up in Palatka and were getting our laundry together when a man strode down the pier to introduce himself and say he'd watched us go past his house on the east side of the river and had to get a closer look. Well, he was an old Navy man who had a little cockle-shell sailboat on shore that he'd rebuilt from splinters, and a thirty-plus-footer behind his house that he was rebuilding. His name was Rit Hinners, and by the time we left the next day, we'd met his wife Betty, they'd carried us to the grocery and postoffice, taken us to see their boats, and had invited us to tie up at their place on our return.

The anchorage we found off Turkey Island north of Welaka was enough to our liking that we dropped the hook there a second time and stayed a few days. Welaka is the self-proclaimed bass capital of the world, though, as I recall, we've caught more bass in Okefenokee. One morning when the sun was glaring across the swamp maples and glaring off the calm waters, I'd turned on the little portable radio to find out whether the world was still in operation. An echoing voice announced, "T minus four and counting." Mary was puttering around in the cockpit making coffee. "Why don't you sorta keep an eye to the southeast. You might, just by chance, see something interesting." She mumbled unintelligibly and went about her chores. Then it was T minus ten seconds. "It's lift off!" It must have been five seconds before Mary saw it. I could tell by the squeaks and gurgles. Rolling out of the bunk, I peered through the door and saw a white plume with a fiery orange object racing skyward ahead of it. By now Mary was looking through the binox and making emotional female noises while I was scrambling for the camera.

Maybe three hundred yards away sat three bass fishermen, tending their lines, backs to the multi-million-dollar fireworks, oblivious to the machinations of science and technology, and all the glory—their floats didn't once quiver. I knew they could hear Mary. Even a great blue heron belly deep on a neighboring lily bed seemed to wonder at her excitement. But this is the essence of fishing: you concentrate on the issue. It takes you out of wonder and worry to a calmness that can be seen best in statues of Buddha. You never see a wrinkle on his forehead; on his belly, yes. *Sylvia II* swung easily as a slight morning breeze ruffled the dark water, swamp water the color of olives. The vapor trails were soon gone, wafted into the wavering cirrus clouds that lay just above the horizon.

From afar we could hear a lawn mower burst into life, accompanied by a barking dog. Then came the scream of a hundred-plus horses thudding a sixteen- to eighteen-foot bass boat downriver towards us. It skittered in a curve across the open water, but the crew must have seen us, for the boat swerved to a stop several yards away. It is a proven fact: if a fisherman sees another fisherman catching a fish, he suspects there must be more fish and will join him, just like gulls on a waterfront. *Sylvia II* rolled and churned in the wake. The blue heron, in apparent disgust, uttered several guttural squawks en route to another lily bed and resettled its plumage.

To fish for bass southern style, first obtain a big—six- to eight-inch— minnow. Hook it through the lips and leave it free to swim on the end of six or eight feet of line. A large float will record any disturbance. Patience is the word. For four hours, three bass boats worked over the grass beds and lily pads beside us. A half-dozen worried the same territory for a couple of hours, and a few, less patient, stirred the neighborhood for upwards of fifteen minutes before moving on. I didn't see a bass caught. Not having the stout tackle of the locals,

I took the flyrod out of the case and attached a popping bug. Mary glanced occasionally at the float marking the drowning location of a worm.

Fly fishing is far ahead of float fishing. At least you are kept busy, selecting new locations and lures, untangling the line from brush and rigging. A sense of skill and artistry comes from arching a lure in long, graceful curves and watching the line unroll across the water and plop a bug alongside a log. A splash; the lure disappears in a swirl of water. A quick set follows, then the quivering tug, line stripping, the steep bow of the rod, and the thrill of line slashing through water.

I shouldn't brag, but at times it's necessary. True, my bream wasn't very big, nor were Mary's that she'd caught on worms. But in a fishing contest we'd have won hands down. The bream weren't much longer than the bait the others were using, but the flavor was better. We could virtually flip our catch aboard and into the ready pan, while the aroma of frying fish drifted past the nostrils of anchored and passing bassmen.

That's the difference between fishermen and amateurs, though there were extenuating circumstances. The bass anglers' downfall, surely, was a bikini occupant, clad mostly in long, flaxen hair. Ostensibly fishing, actually she was sunbathing. Any average bass fisherman, not being a purist, was diverted from his real purpose and anchored close to catch the action. The only true fishermen were the three early birds: when the space shuttle went up, they saw nothing; when water skiers streaked by, they saw nothing; when the bikini paused nearby, they saw nothing.

~~~~~~~~~~~~~~~~~~~~~~~~

Though credited to Paul Bunyan, that mythical logger from the North Woods, the legend of Round River has been given added meaning by the distinguished conservationist Aldo Leopold. Round River is a mighty river that flows into itself and runs in a big circle, never ending, maybe never exactly beginning. No matter; man's nature, it seems, is always to try to change things. Not that change is bad, nor necessarily good. But man, being by his own reckoning smartest of all creatures, at times produces some wonderfully contrasting results.

Like all rivers except Round River, the waters of the St. Johns rise in the uplands, among swamps and springs, forests and bogs. A puddling spring gathers itself together and meanders to the nearest low spot, pools, perhaps even forming a lake or two, then finds its way to join other such waters. Lakes give birth to rivers, providing habitat for birds, alligators, turtles, snakes, manatees, and many other forms of life that the Lord put on earth, it is said, for man to hold dominion over; for man, it is said also, is to be the steward. The problem with words like "steward" and "stewardship" is that lots of otherwise intelligent folk don't know what they mean. Their interpretation seems to reflect the attitude of the old river pirates, whose motto was, Take what you can and the Devil take the hindmost.

As with all rivers, man wants a change, but he usually wants to alter for selfish motives, though he will not admit it. The farmer wants more land so that he can "feed the world." Actually, he wants more crops to increase his income. Nothing wrong with that. The forester wants more timber, so that people can build homes and have plenty of paper. The truth is, the forester does not really care about the end result. He, too, is looking for more profit. And there is nothing wrong with that. Then there is the developer, who wants to change this wasteland, this useless swamp, into productive land. The Chamber of Commerce and the county commissioners nod in agreement, for this means more people and more business, and it will "keep our young people at home." And, ah yes, more taxes, so they can have a new courthouse—the old one's getting rather seedy—and another secretary, so that more of the commissioners' time can be devoted to the people's problems. Now how can anyone find fault with that?

The St. Johns is a system, from its billions of blind mosquitoes, so thick at times one can scarcely breathe, to the fisherman; from its sweetwater springs to its oil barges, southbound full, northbound empty, that fill the narrows from bank to bank. One source estimates the economic return of the fishing world alone at an excess of seven hundred million dollars a year, fifty million of that just in fishing rod and reel sales. But there is the old quarrel of land use. Jacksonville sailor Phil Thibodeau is deeply interested in the river. He agrees that if the developers who benefit from the diversion of the headwaters had to pay for the damage they have done, and restore the habitat they blithely rearranged, their ventures would not have been profitable. "You bet they'd be running to the courts with their lawyers, yelling 'Foul!' Yet they have criminally fouled our river and got away with it."

Waterfront developments, in the form of twin-tower, twelve- to twenty-story condos, are beginning to crowd the shoreline. A developer gets a small piece of river frontage, builds towers blocking the rest of the city's view and access with private facilities. What happens behind the towers? A slum, a ghetto, as has occurred in many cities in the past, like Miami Beach, where muggings and other crimes continue to rise.

At one landing, where we'd pulled in for ice, two men were discussing the river. "It's those ranchers," declared one; "they have tremendous holdings mid-state, got the land cheap, and today they hold the key." "They're so powerful you can't fight 'em, yet they're the ones who drain the land to get more pasture and cropland," said the other. "They say to hell with the rest of the people. To them this river is a big sewer for their use." An engineer spoke up, suggesting a lock on the river to keep out the salt water, because "you'll never stop the drainage." At a marina near Sanford another opinion was offered, "We need a couple or three real good hurricanes. It'll raise the water level and bring the land back to life. Those turkeys who are developing never had to go through a hurricane. Might take a little profit out of it for them." Nearly everyone we met on the river expressed similar opinions, differing solutions about the river that is narrow between lakes, with green walls of vegetation, twisting and turning bends and curves, islands of floating rafts of hyacinths.

Interrupting my thoughts is an osprey, hovering high overhead. It hangs, sharply black and white, against a blue sky spattered with small, puffy white clouds. The bird's broad shoulders suggest power and speed. Suddenly it plummets, a guided missile. A shower of spray explodes as it strikes with tremendous force, emerging with a fish in its talons. Quickly it rises high again, shuddering the water from its feathers on to *Sylvia II* and flying to the top of a dead cypress. The osprey, like the pelican, has made a remarkable comeback. A bird that was abundant in the 1940s had virtually disappeared from this country by the mid-fifties and sixties. Since the controlling of chlorinated hydrocarbons such as DDT, the species has been gradually restored and now is becoming almost common in scattered areas.

Everything man does comes back to him in some form. The drainage of Jersey and Florida swamps made more land, raised taxes, and caused more suburbia; but the price? Well, it reduced the fresh water recharging capabilities on which all who lived there were dependent, and as the fresh water supply was reduced, salt water replaced it. The problem of excess fresh water for a few became a lack of fresh water for many. By providing more land to develop in return, the demand for fresh water increased.

On this river, where our boat skates about her anchor in the freshening afternoon breeze that sets a little chop against the current, we consider its sources. A thousand springs and swamps? Perhaps ten thousand. As each swamp is conquered and converted, it is no longer a source. And the five-foot tide of the Atlantic pushes farther upstream, until blue crabs can be caught seventy-five miles inland and more. The St. Johns is probably one of the greatest fresh water fishing areas in all of America. It is without doubt one of the best reservoirs of wildlife in the southeast, the last sanctuary of the manatee, once found as far north as New Jersey, where the last one sighted was about to give birth when some louts from Brielle were able to conquer the species there by clubbing, stabbing, and shooting, some thirty-five years ago.

This river, still healthy, does show signs of distress, but not by deliberate destruction. The Cross-Florida Barge Canal, a monument to man's craving to alter the environment, has choked off and diverted millions of gallons of fresh water. Drainage canals bypassing the river have contributed to the problems; various state and federal agencies, all through public funds, have had their effect. These efforts have helped a few to profit, but the cost has been high, not only in dollars but in the effects on the rest of the land. It's a Round River here, too.

~~~~~~~~~~~~~~~~~~~~~~

I'll not soon forget the morning I heard this strangled cry from Mary: "Good God! Good God!" I left the wheel and spun around: "What's the matter?" Had the coffee boiled over? Binoculars in one hand, she was pointing into the dense cypress swamps that fringe the St. Johns.

"Well what did you expect me to say, 'Pileated woodpecker! Pileated woodpecker!' I got your attention, didn't I?"

I held my tongue and put the boat back on course. This is the sort of thing a man must expect to put up with when he allows women to come along to cook, make up bunks and attend to other shipboard details, instead of staying home and bringing in a regular paycheck as a well-trained female should. Still, come wintertime, there are very few places to equal the bird watching potential of central Florida. And there is a thrill, maybe a bit of nostalgia, when one sees again those rare and endangered species that have come close to becoming extinct. The osprey is returning. The brown pelican, that had reached a low of only one surviving nestling from thousands of nesting pairs, is gaining in healthy numbers. The peregrine falcon has been seen again along the Atlantic seaboard. Until about ten years ago there hadn't been a successful nesting of bald eagles in North Carolina in at least two decades. Since then, as many as four eagles have been sighted on the coast. On the St. Johns we saw two, an adult and a juvenile. Wildlife populations are a revealing indicator of the health of the nation, for if wildlife cannot survive, there is something wrong. Man, despite his prejudices, depends on the same animal needs of soil, air, and water quality that perpetuate other species.

The St. Johns being the center of the bass fishing world, we dropped rods and tackle box into our inflatable, and I yanked the starter cord of the little outboard, which plopped to life at once. The raft undulated over the waves, nudged through the hyacinths upstream to where the fish were waiting. "Eat your hearts out, you bass fishermen—a real pro is on his way," I mused smugly to myself. The river was a stained brown, but a clear streak entered from a tributary, so we meandered up to where a fence blocked the entrance. A sign proclaimed, "No motors beyond this point." Mary took the oars while I probed the shore and holes for fish. It was a good-sized bream that took the lure, and I was fighting it to a standstill, with wife making encouraging noises, when I happened to look beneath us. A great monster, longer than our twelve-foot raft, was stirring, rising towards us. Forgetting the fish, I pointed at the creature: the size of a small hippo, dull gray with a tail like a beaver, two small forearms, a lumpy head and a nose more bulbous than W. C. Fields', its bewhiskered face looked up at us, beady black eyes half hidden in rolls of flesh. It rolled to the surface, sniffed at us and sounded, but slowly: a manatee, the mermaid of yesteryear, when sailors had stronger drinks and were away from port longer. Across its back were slash scars where propellers had hit. Here, another endangered species once known in North Carolina, making its final stand in south central Florida.

Hundreds of thousands, even millions, of gallons a day come from the underground river that is the source of Blue Spring Run. Tasting the water, we detected a slight trace of salt. If so, the warnings of the people are well founded. The tug of the ocean can be felt as far upriver as Hontoon Island, about 150 miles from the sea, leaving but a thin layer of fresh water to supply the needs of millions of people for their land, farms, drinking, and industrial supply.

There are two kinds of folks who hang out on the water. For lack of a better designation, we'll call them boatmen and boaters. Boatmen are those who seem to fit in with the waterways, like a soft shoe. Everyone knows the breed: the old fisherman with his aging backyard-built boat, who knows every ripple, lump, and slough. Especially around the Chesapeake, he's called a waterman, which implies he knows what he's about when he boards a boat. We can include many of a wealthier class, those who have been cruising for years with their mahogany and polished brass and teak-trimmed custom-built yachts. Many of them, too, have a love, respect, and feel for the waterways and fit with the environment.

But lately there has been a rash of what may best be termed boaters, so named by the admen who don't know that a boater is an old-fashioned straw hat. The new breed has sprung up, a by-product of our recent and, some believe, soon-to-be-departed affluence. They carry an infectious disease that has spread into all areas of the water world. They judge a boat by the number of people it sleeps. If they had ever slept on a troop ship, they'd know better. It is possible, in those hell holes, to pack almost any body in an eighteen-inch by twelve-inch by (skimpy) six-foot box quite easily, by stomping hard enough. But should that be the criterion? The next standard of the boater is power. If some is good, more is better. If ten horsepower is enough, then twenty must be better, so let's make it two hundred and be sure. After all, it makes more noise and that's good. Sadly, modern-day bass fishermen have fallen into this trap.

Now fishing is an honorable sport, and it rates among the top. Most fishermen are also the ultimate in manhood, gentlemen of the first order, but they have been sold a bill of goods. In order to fish for bass today, one must join a club. But this is not necessarily bad, for almost all the real leadership in conservation has come from clubs. Then one must have a boat. Okay so far, but no longer can one fish from a row skiff, or even a john boat. He must have a bass boat with a swivel chair, a console, upholstered floors—no, I didn't mean to say decks—circulating tanks, and enough horsepower to fly (many aircraft have less). Until you have clung to the swivel chair, slamming across a little chop, ears flapping, teeth clattering, blinded by the slipstream, you cannot be considered a real bass fisherman. Ah yes, and the appropriate costume is a jump suit, which the unreconstructed boatman still calls coveralls.

Imagine twenty or thirty or forty of these boats in a fishing contest—for competition is the name of the game—at fifty mph on your pond, without traffic lights or even cops. It's like holding the

Indianapolis 500 in a parking lot. I've tried it, and I get so shook I can't even tie a lure to the line. These bass boys are so numb they could thread a hawser through a sewing needle in a hurricane. They should get a medal for heroism. Somehow the lazy river, the bank shaded by moss-covered live oaks, the flipping of a lure among lily pads, all are lost in the flying spume of racing boats. And it's not just bass fishermen. It's everywhere in leisure living.

The economical, comfortable displacement boat is passé. Wood is outmoded: no longer the mellowness of teak and mahogany, the sweet smell of juniper and cypress, the strength and resilience of oak, the tradition of heart pine. Georgia gave the frigate *Constitution* her original oak timbers; today there is not an oak in all of Georgia to repair *Old Ironsides*. Today it is more a plastic mania, cold, hard, greasy-smooth moulds. The smell of tar and turpentine is gone. The craze for speed has replaced the rewards of observation.

Sylvia II is one of the mellow boats of quality, capable of handling almost anything thrown at her in her dignified way. Throughout our waterway passage she has cruised, solid and stable in wind, rain, and fair weather, while we stood or sat on deck watching the birds feeding along the banks, her wake but a whisper among the roots and grasses of the shoreline. Yet whenever we tied up for the night and visited with neighboring boat crews, most seemed to be hung on a similar tune, "Yep, we cruised the Waterway—only took us four days." We'd already taken weeks and hadn't got to the turning around point yet.

One evening we found ourselves in a sea of houseboats, aluminum and plastic. The owner of a neighboring chromed barge left his color TV superwide screen and peered out at us. "Came down the St. Johns, eh? I did it, too, averaged forty miles an hour. Pretty, ain't it?" He couldn't have had time to see the tree with the anhinga poised, drying its wet plumage. Of course he missed the osprey that had dived to lift a trout from the backwaters and retired to feed from a vantage point high in a great cypress. How could he have watched the water boiling up from an underground spring, bright green, and the schools of fish? What chance was there for him to visit with anchored skiff fishermen dropping flies expertly among the lily pads, or to stop at small villages and explore their dusty side streets? I guess that the difference between boatmen and boaters is that some folks just don't have time to enjoy their leisure.

The wide flow of one of America's larger rivers is dark from the acids of its tupelo- and cypress-rich banks. Its edges are jade green with water hyacinths, beneath the long-limbed giants draped with the gray green of Spanish moss. Bass and alligators are both legendary and real. Some villages can still be called sleepy, and the towns along its banks, as well as the creeks and rivers that feed it, have Indian names. On the St. Johns are palmetto scrub and rattlesnakes, armadillos and citrus trees, moss-slick docks and mouldering fish camps. And hyacinths. The St. Johns is knee-deep in them. Outboards struggle through them hopelessly. A huge mat of them is a Sargasso Sea to small boating. Surely there sits, in a vast pond of shining green hyacinths, the rusting remnants of an outboard motor, its operator reduced to a cob-webbed skeleton forever entrapped by the nemesis of freshwater Florida.

<hr/>

At just about the time black night was merging with the deep blue-gray of pre-sunrise, I first heard it, a sound like rain sweeping across the water. I rolled over, still mostly asleep. Maybe it would go away. But the noise intensified, as if it were coming from beneath the boat. Curiosity overcame laziness, and I fumbled through the mosquito net snapped to the cabin door. Peering over the side, I saw the water bubbling furiously along the waterline, with tiny flashes of silver and an occasional larger boil. Fingerling shad by the thousands were feeding on the windrows of mosquitoes lodged at the waterline, and bass were dining on the shad. A clump of hyacinths drifted by, it too boiling with feeding fish. The last stars faded. Gray-to-black clouds lay along a horizon of pines and palmettoes. On a neighboring shore, standing among the aquatic plants, more than a hundred herons and egrets were lined up at water's edge, and they were gorging on the fish rise.

The air was still cool and damp when Mary joined me to watch the birds, and the sky was reddening to the east. With slow majesty a red orb poked through the clouds. We could see it move, turning from red to orange to yellow, then to the white fireball of semi-tropical skies as a new day began. I pumped up the pressure on the stove while Mary prepared the coffee pot. As she continued the breakfast routine, I manned the swab, listening to an owl still calling from a patch of woods nearby. Red-winged blackbirds and grackles flitted noisily, and grebes dove in panic at the sight of me.

Mary had just settled with toast and coffee when something caught her eye. There, silent and still, six or eight feet from her, was a big alligator, its knobby nose and protruding eyes just above the water. It watched her steadily. We watched, wondering. Then with scarcely a ripple, it disappeared into the dark depths. It came again at noon, and at sundown, always appearing without warning and fading imperceptibly, like dissipating smoke. Said Mary, "I have the feeling that Nautilus is coming and James Mason is driving."

For several days we lazied in this anchorage, routinely fishing, sunbathing, reading, and dreaming. Though we never fed it, the alligator seemed to know whenever a meal was being prepared. Morning, noon, and evening it would emerge silently, seldom more than two or three yards away, regarding us with those dark, unblinking reptilian eyes. I doubt that it would have taken much effort for it to come over the low freeboard of the boat had it wanted to do so, yet it never bothered us, never made an aggressive move. It just waited, hopefully, I suppose, for a handout—it could make a man nervous.

So, it had started when we commiserated with Cap'n Theodore. That led to a four-hundred dollar boat that required almost a year of part-time work and, I figured, around twelve hundred dollars to restore the old craft. It took a great deal of labor, too, on the part of Mary and me, but that was the fun, what made it all come together. Oh yes, we'd had to build that thirty-eight-dollar dock for her, too. All in all, a great education. For someone else it might never be worth the effort, yet today she gets more compliments than any of her neighbors, and to cruise her is a delight.

At 7.8 knots she requires sixteen hundred of her maximum thirty-six hundred rpm with a 2:1 reduction and a big wheel. Her smooth lines and easy riding give us six miles to the gallon. Despite her narrow beam, by today's standards her roll is easy, not excessive. She lifts well to a sea, yet knifes through without a lot of bobble. She's tight and dry, and her handling is a dream: set the rudder amidships after aiming her, and, if she drifts slightly, just step to the side and she'll change course. We've cruised several miles without need of touching the wheel, yet her big screw and counter-balanced rudder will spin her in about twice her length. She'll pull a trawl, yet one can work her in less than waist-deep water with no problems. It's easy to haul a net aboard, and she makes a perfect swimming platform, with no real need for a boarding ladder.

But even lolling in the warm winter sun of Florida, with graceful palms framing every picturebook scene, skitter boats speeding by, bikinis and orange trees all about, we realize that this is not quite the place for *Sylvia II*. She belongs in those clear green Carolina waters, where the southwest trades sweep sweet and bear the tang of salt. She needs to feel the tug of the inlets and follow the channels that spread like the footprint of a big bird where sea and sound meet. She must be anchored again in the backwaters on cold winter days where the wild goose can be heard. Her world is on the ocean swells rising in Onslow Bay under the watchful eye of the diving tern as she circles a school of mackerel, for she's Carolina born and bred and that is where she belongs.

If some cool winter day you happen upon a classy antique anchored in a cove and catch the aromas of frying fish, hot biscuits, and maybe clam chowder wafting across the water, you can expect to see a fellow with his feet up and a smile on his face, because he made a real good deal.